NUMEROLOGY

NUMEROLOGY

A Guide to Decoding Your Destiny with the Hidden Meaning of Numbers

Anne-Sophie Casper

STERLING ETHOS

New York

STERLING ETHOS
New York

Illustrations and French text © 2022 Secret d'étoiles Éditions, Paris
English translation © 2024 Sterling Publishing Co., Inc.

ISBN 978-1-4549-5083-7
ISBN 978-1-4549-5084-4 (e-book)

Library of Congress Control Number: 2023938588

For information about custom editions, special sales, and premium purchases,
please contact specialsales@unionsquareandco.com.

Printed in China

2 4 6 8 10 9 7 5 3 1

unionsquareandco.com

Cover and interior design by Julie Mathieu
Translation by Chloe Zarka Grinsnir

To all the people who matter
to me and all the people I can
rely on, like my faithful and
precious friend Pouce, who
will recognize herself!

To all the people who think
they're just one little number
among many.

CONTENTS

"All things are numbers."

—PYTHAGORAS

PREFACE

I'VE BEEN CAPTIVATED by words ever since I've known how to read and write. I've always been more comfortable around literature than I've been around mathematics. For years, I carefully kept numbers and anything related to mathematics at bay. At the tender age of ten, I had already figured out any tricks and subterfuges imaginable so I wouldn't have to learn how to do long division by hand. Twenty-seven years later, I still don't know how to do it! But not to worry . . . I'm very happy living like this.

Comforted by the limitations I had (either inherited or created), I was completely stuck. The door leading to calculus was locked. When thinking about numbers, I always immediately perceived them as colors, or as colorful words. The numerical aspect of numbers confused me, blurred in my brain. Even for someone as sharp minded as me, solving equations and arithmetic exams proved to be challenging. I often disguised my bad mathematics grades out of pride, soon becoming an expert in forging my parents' signature.

It wasn't until I turned thirty-one that life allowed me to better understand my differences. Only then did I manage to pick the locks of this intellectual fortress. I allowed myself to let go by looking at numbers differently. I was surprised to see how quickly I understood things, but more importantly, how much fun I had practicing math in my own way. The Universe then gave me signs, all directly connected to the practice of numerology. Encounters, books, conferences, training . . . my incredible journey through the land of numbers was already enhancing my everyday life. And yet, it had just begun. And here I am a few years down the line, asked to write an introductory guide to numerology, then this book, which provides more detail on the subject. Who, knowing the hate I used to feel for numbers as a kid, could have thought this would happen? Thanks to numerology, numbers have given me so much. Truly, anything is possible!

Numerology is a powerful tool for self-development and a wonderful way to learn more about oneself. This method touches the most intimate parts of ourselves, our essence and our identity. Numerology gives tangible answers to help us develop our gifts and turn them into talents. We only need a few pieces of information (name, family name, and date of birth) for numerology to unveil our personalities, our achievements, our potential, our strengths and challenges. However, let's not forget that nothing and no one can access absolute truth, not even numerology. It is not an exact science, because there is no standardization of the results we obtain through numerology.

> **FREE WILL** The information I reveal in this book is always dependent on your free will and is never meant to be seen as a set of hard and fast rules with immutable answers. This is subjective information with no predetermined meaning. It is simply advice that may resonate within you. Your responsibility and autonomy are always essential in interpreting the information I am about to share.

When my editor offered me a chance to share my approach of numerology with people, it was critical for me to outline not only what I call rational numerology but also intuitive numerology.

Rational numerology is intimately connected to the brain's left hemisphere, the center for logic, analytical thinking, and rationality. It is the method most seen in books about numerology, and it uses simple mathematical equations.

On the other hand, I associate **intuitive numerology** with the brain's right hemisphere. Just like this part of the brain, it is creative, holistic, and intuitive, and so it's rarely used in numerology books out of fear of lacking seriousness. Thoughts are treated globally and not in a sequential way. That's why I offer an intuitive approach of numerology through tests.

The two hemispheres complete each other perfectly. As you're about to see, their functions are completely adapted to the discovery, understanding, practice, and learning of numerology.

I wish you all a beautiful exploration and a wonderful practice.

SOME IMPORTANT NOTIONS TO GET STARTED

Single Digits or Double Digits?

To perform a numerical analysis, you need to associate both single- and double-digit numbers. I believe there is a great difference between them. Numbers measure quantity, but single-digit numbers from 1 to 9 are the graphic and aesthetic symbols that represent the numbers. However, numerology dives into the symbolic aspect of numbers and not their aesthetic aspect. This is why I will treat both single- and double-digit numbers the same way, as numbers, as it is customary in numerology.

We Can Only Control the Present

It is impossible to change our past. The same is true of our future—it will only outline itself after we make our various life choices. Thanks to numerology, we can tangibly act on the present, the here and the now, in order to create a more harmonious, balanced, and flourishing near future. Thus, it is essential to respect the free will, autonomy, and personal responsibility of every person wishing to use the tool of numerology. For moral and ethical reasons, it is also crucial to always ask for someone's permission before doing numerology work about them. If you wish to offer someone a numerology analysis, you must first discreetly make sure that it is an appropriate gift, like you would do with any other surprise gift.

Numerology Is Not Trivial

Numerology is serious business, hence the importance of asking for permission before anything else. With the exception of particular cases, I do not recommend using numerology with babies, young children, and kids under sixteen. In my opinion, numerology could affect the unconscious brain of the parents and other guardians, thus influencing the life of the young "consultant" (see the little lexicon of numerology on p. 26). Let's give these young beings (sometimes only a few weeks old) the freedom to tame the world they just arrived in.

1

EXPLORE
YOUR BRAIN

✦

I N THIS FIRST chapter, let's review some things together. Are you ready to explore your brain? Take this quiz to find out and help you develop the two hemispheres of your brain (the left and the right), both useful in numerology.

First, I have some advice that should be easy for you to apply to your practice.

Additionally, I will be answering the question "What is numerology, exactly?" Do you know its history, origins, and various applications?

Take your time reading this first chapter. It answers so many questions. Be mindful of your breathing as you take in all the concepts discussed here. Let this new information infuse you and allow it to help you understand.

ARE YOU READY TO EXPLORE YOUR BRAIN?

✦

I should warn you, exploring your brain is not without consequences. You will have to step out of your comfort zone and experience many surprises, discoveries, and challenges. To confirm that you are ready to begin this experience and to help you feel ready, I invite you to answer the four questions below. The first two questions are dedicated to the left hemisphere and the other two are dedicated to the right hemisphere.

TEST YOURSELF!

Take a deep breath and calmly read the following affirmations. In complete honesty and transparency with yourself, select the sentences that apply to you. Calculate the total for each question, sum up the first two numbers, then the other two, and discover your result. Let's go!

LEFT BRAIN

Question 1: My Personality and My Emotions

☐ I am a rational person, rather stubborn and with very strong opinions.
☐ People say I am very talkative.
☐ I like to express myself, especially through writing (letters, emails, lists . . .).
☐ I like words, but I also don't hate math!
☐ I always favor reflection, action, and know-how.
☐ I have a great capacity for analysis (about projects, people, places, situations . . .).
☐ I am logical; I appreciate accuracy, tangible information, and facts.
☐ I can sometimes be inflexible about seemingly trivial details.
☐ I think it's important to fulfill our own needs before thinking about someone else's.
☐ I am very reasonable, and nothing can make me forget my sense of reality.

TOTAL 1 = ...

Question 2: My Hobbies and Passions

☐ I like to understand, think, analyze, and dissect information.
☐ I love puzzles, rebus, and riddles.
☐ I like individual sports (tennis, fencing, table tennis, badminton . . .).
☐ I feel right at home during an escape game.
☐ I like to discover and practice new methods to better know and surpass myself, and thus evolve.
☐ I am passionate about history and anything related to it (museums, monuments . . .).
☐ I fluently speak many foreign languages.
☐ I never lack ideas and energy, which allow me to plan big projects.
☐ I am usually the designated planner for parties and events.

TOTAL 2 = ...

TOTAL 1 + 2 = ...

LEFT BRAIN KEYWORDS

ATTENTION TO DETAIL

SEQUENTIAL THINKING

COMMITMENT TO THE FACTS

LINEAL ANALYTICAL PROCESSING

LOGICAL AND IDEA-RICH MIND

LEFT BRAIN RESULTS

If you have selected 16 or more affirmations, you make the most of your left hemisphere. You're ready—more than ready, even—to explore rational numerology. Be grateful for what pushed you to read this book, for you possess all the essential tools to calmly explore rational numerology. A little reminder: as you read this book, remember to respect your own personal rhythm so you can fully experience your discoveries. The integration must be done step by step. To preserve your left brain and feed your soul, look at my recommendations on p. 18.

If you have selected from 8 to 15 affirmations, well done! It seems you possess a great base, solid and strong, to begin this beautiful adventure. You have all the tools needed to optimize how you utilize your left brain, especially if the totals for each of the two questions are similar. If they aren't, I advise you to focus primarily on areas that you feel compelled to improve, such as your personality and emotions, or your hobbies and passions. You will earn more confidence and balance, which will help you explore rational numerology more calmly.

If you have selected 7 affirmations or fewer, I invite you to deeply question yourself, without any judgment. On a scale of 0 to 10, how are you feeling right now? If curiosity and joy are still motivating you, don't give up. Remind yourself of the reasons that pushed you to open this book. Why is it important to you to discover rational numerology? To reach your goal, take action by trying out my suggestions on the following pages. Take the time to assimilate them and respect your rhythm. Stay confident and let go. If this is your path, the time you take to explore it is irrelevant. The ideal moment will come, be it an hour, a day, or a year.

MY ADVICE ON DEVELOPING THE
LEFT HEMISPHERE OF YOUR BRAIN

If you still need to cultivate your left brain through precision and rationalization, look on the bright side: you're one of a rare group of people with a stronger right hemisphere! Take advantage of this uniqueness and turn it into an asset. For too long, our society has valued logical thinking, neglecting the concepts of intuition, creativity, and holistic vision.

Play with Words

To juggle words as well as creative ideas, practice word associations as fast as you can, alone or with other people. For instance, if I say the word music, what immediately comes to mind? Personally, I instantly think about the words conservatory, instrument, score, and note. This type of word association is purely logical and mental. It does not make use of your feelings or emotions.

Play with Numbers

Following the example of the word association, dedicate time to having fun solving mathematical or logical riddles. To make the game more exciting, try playing with other people in teams. To experiment on your own, have a game of chess against your computer or fill out several pages of sudoku puzzles.

Develop Your Memory

To cultivate your ability to easily memorize things, take the contact list from your phone and pick the first phone number you see. At your pace, try learning the numbers by memorizing them in pairs. The next day, as you wake up, try remembering the whole phone number. As soon as you've memorized it, try another one. Then try the same exercise with names and family names. To memorize the names and information of people outside your immediate social group, try committing social media handles to memory or study magazines and websites about celebrity gossip until you are able to easily identify anyone who is profiled there.

Make Lists

Having the general idea for a project or for what you want to do in a day is important. But if you don't have all the different steps in mind (and the right order for them), it's useless. A piece of advice to structure yourself: make lists! Create a monthly to-do list and organize each task by order of importance and urgency. It will help you stay organized, manage your priorities, and improve your memory. Every time you accomplish a task, checking or crossing it off a list will give you a sense of progress and accomplishment.

Channel Your Ideas

To remember all the thoughts crossing your mind, I recommend writing in an idea notebook or using your phone's recorder as you dictate your ideas. You'll quickly get the ideas out of your system so you can come back to them later. You can then more easily focus on more urgent matters without needlessly cluttering your brain. As someone who multitasks a lot, I like using colored notebooks, Post-it notes, and memos to avoid getting my projects mixed up.

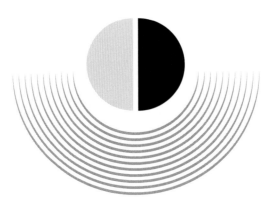

RIGHT BRAIN

Question 3: My Personality and My Emotions

☐ People say I'm curious, open-minded, and original but also easily swayed.

☐ I am spontaneous and genuine, but I can be too impulsive sometimes.

☐ I'm empathetic, but my (hyper) sensitivity can often play tricks on me!

☐ I'm very romantic.

☐ I have the soul of an artist, and always rely on my intuition.

☐ I'm great at connecting ideas, people, things, and situations.

☐ I listen to my body, and I express the emotions I feel.

☐ I believe it's very important to always favor collaboration and the community.

☐ My thoughts are tree-structured, and I have a great visual memory.

☐ I'm a passionate person and I always react intensely (in joy and sorrow).

TOTAL 3 = ...

Question 4: My Hobbies and Passions

☐ I have a vivid imagination.

☐ I like to play or listen to music.

☐ I have at least two artistic gifts (drawing, painting, sculpting, acting, photography, scrapbooking, pottery, dancing, etc.).

☐ I love mystery stories and unsolved cases.

☐ I follow my instincts when it comes to picking a hobby or a travel destination.

☐ I'm very athletic.

☐ I've always enjoyed art, no matter the medium.

☐ I love telling stories, true or made-up.

☐ I'm a very social person, and I enjoy family meetings and friends' gatherings.

☐ I sing everyday (under the shower, in my bedroom, or with my children).

TOTAL 4 = ...

TOTAL 3 + 4 =.............

RIGHT BRAIN KEYWORDS

DEVELOPED INTUITION AND EMOTIONS

IMAGINATIVE AND ARTISTIC APPROACH

CREATIVE REASONING

CLEAR VISION OF A GOAL

GLOBAL AND HOLISTIC PROCESSING

RIGHT BRAIN RESULTS

If you have selected 16 or more affirmations, your right brain is rich and perfectly nourished—well done! The timing for beginning your study is perfect. Give thanks to life, for you are ready to approach intuitive numerology. However, don't skip any of the steps outlined in this book. I would advise you to really respect your personal rhythm in order to fully enjoy your discoveries. As with a good tea, let the information infuse your mind so it can be fully integrated. To preserve the richness of your right brain and feed your creative mind, take a look at my recommendations below.

If you have selected from 8 to 15 affirmations, you have a solid base for studying. You can rely on the power and the strength of your right brain to explore intuitive numerology. You possess all the essential tools to develop the positive aspects of your right brain, especially if the totals for each of the two questions are similar. If they aren't yet, I would advise you to focus on the advice about the themes where you scored the lowest. You'll then feel more confident about discovering and practicing

the techniques I will be sharing in this book.

If you have selected 7 affirmations or fewer, I invite you to deeply question yourself, without any judgment. On a scale of 0 to 10, how are you feeling right now? If curiosity and joy are still motivating you, don't give up. Remind yourself of the reasons that pushed you to open this book. Why is it important to you to discover intuitive numerology? To reach your goal, take action by trying out my suggestions on the following pages. Take the time to assimilate them and respect your rhythm. Stay confident and let go. If this is your path, the time you take to explore it is irrelevant. The ideal moment will come—be it in an hour, a day, or a year.

MY ADVICE ON DEVELOPING THE RIGHT

HEMISPHERE OF YOUR BRAIN

Faced with the powerful and imposing left brain, our right hemisphere may struggle to measure up. Naturally less developed, it is yet dedicated to essential things like empathy, wisdom, sensitivity, socialization, nonverbal analysis, intuition, and creativity. And Jill Bolte Taylor won't contradict me. After a stroke in 1996, all the functions of her left brain were "frozen." That's when the scientist, who specialized in neuroanatomy, discovered the potential of the other hemisphere. To discover her story, I invite you to watch the TED Talk she gave on the subject in February 2008.

Open Yourself to the World

To understand the world, plan at least one cultural outing per month, as well as an artistic activity, with family or friends. Open your mind by opening your eyes. Sharpen your curiosity by developing your five senses. An experience lived by your right hemisphere will be intimately connected to your feelings and sensations. Get lost in a new place—or even online—like you would in the unknown streets of a village during a trip. Opening the doors to unusual places will favor new encounters and thus new experiences. Try a new bar or restaurant you've been wanting to sample for months, or take a new path to work or school. At the same time, you will develop your empathy, and understand more easily the differences between cultures, religions, traditions, ways of working, and so on.

Give Things Meaning

To be inspired and inspiring, your mind must awaken. One of the ways to do it is to touch your heart and your spirit. To do so, you must think and act with meaning. As with the beliefs that forge your being, this meaning is yours alone to determine. This quality is neither logical nor rational. For instance, some will feel alive and energized in the middle of a crowd during a concert, others while playing their favorite sports for hours, or still others—like me—while creating art quietly in the quiet of their own bedroom. As I write these words, I am filled with gratitude while watching the Saint Lawrence River, surrounded by squirrels, sparrows, and seagulls. Essentially what you are working toward is the cohesion of your thoughts and your actions. You cannot give your life meaning if your thoughts and words are dissonant with what you do. So, (re)connect yourself to your deepest aspirations, dreams, and wishes—they will always bring you meaning.

Listen and Imagine

Listen to conversations on the train. Observe people in waiting rooms Look at how your pets behave. All these things are an inexhaustible source of creative matter for your imagination. If you can't make up stories about what you see, begin by writing a few lines in a notebook each day. These writings will remain secret and private. No one but you will read them. Let your ideas flow, create them, modify them, and enrich the characters and backgrounds in which they evolve.

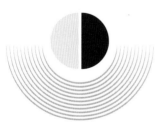

Keep in mind that no idea is wrong or bad. Each idea deserves to be thought and thus to exist.

Unveil Your Feelings

If you're not used to sharing how you feel or saying loudly and clearly what you feel, or if you're uncomfortable unveiling your emotions, this exercise might seem unsurmountable at first glance. But it's not. As with any other goal, you need to figure out steps that will thwart the obstacles you'll face. These steps will help you express yourself without pressuring yourself.

Step 1: Start by mentally questioning how you're feeling. Don't think, but rather rely on your five senses to determine your inner state. The clearer it is, the easier it will be to share so that what you feel can be heard and understood.

Step 2: Before your left brain has a chance to start working, express your state without any pressure or limitations.

Step 3: Your left brain, should it catch up, may not feel the same way. It doesn't matter at all. No one can deny how you're feeling. You are the only one feeling it.

Step 4: Question yourself about what you just went through. Meditate on this experience, and practice letting go.

Play and Create

In each and every one of us, there is an inner child, waiting to be summoned to play. Without having to return to kindergarten, I'm advising you to do things seriously without taking yourself too seriously. Use all your serious adult responsibilities as a chance to have fun. Your chores or accounting must be done, so why not turn these boring moments into pleasurable moments through dancing or singing? Playing will allow you to combine business with pleasure.

IF YOU HAD SIMILAR RESULTS It's pretty rare, but if, like me, your left brain's results are very close to your right brain's results, I have a little exercise for you. It will help you determine your dominant hemisphere. In the example below, do you instinctively read the words or see the colors? If you read the words first, your left brain is dominant. If you see the colors first, your right brain is dominant.

BLACK   BLUE   GREEN

WHITE   GREEN   RED

GREEN   PURPLE   YELLOW

YELLOW   PINK   OCHRE

RED   YELLOW   WHITE

WHAT IS NUMEROLOGY, EXACTLY?

✦

A LITTLE LEXICON OF NUMEROLOGY

When it comes to advice in the realm of personal development and spirituality, I often notice drifts, contradictions, and approximations in the language of many books. I believe it is absolutely necessary to use the correct professional terms. It doesn't matter if the audience is composed of neophytes or experts. That is why it seems important for me to share relevant theoretical notions with you, even if you are just discovering numerology. I deeply believe that words have power and impact, whether they are being spoken, written, or read. I have a keen interest in their symbolism, their precision, and their accuracy, and you will find below a little (non-exhaustive) lexicon of numerology. It contains the main terms used in the third part of this book. I invite you to refer to it as you read.

ARITHMANCY

1	2	3	4	5	6	7	8	9
A	B	C	D	E	F	G	H	I
J	K	L	M	N	O	P	Q	R
S	T	U	V	W	X	Y	Z	

This method is inextricably linked to the Pythagorean alphabet (see Pythagorean Alphabet), also called Tripoli's alphabet. Thanks to it, we can make numerous operations whose results are important bases in numerology (active number,

hereditary number, expressive number, spiritual momentum, intimate self, etc.; see p. 29).

CONSULTANT

The term consultant is commonly used in numerology to refer to the person for whom the numerological research is performed. It is derived from the idea that one consults a numerologist, like you would consult an astrologer or a medium.

F

FAMILY NAME

Far from being trivial, our family name represents our family's heredity. It typically refers to the father's heritage, for he is often the one passing down his name, but if you are taking another family member's last name, this would represent their attendant heritage. This includes all family principles and values handed down to us. But what we get through this family name isn't always what we keep or mainly develop through our life. Some people take everything; others reject it entirely or only keep a piece of it.

KARMIC DEBT

The term debt is borrowed from the field of accounting. In transgenerational numerology (or the numerology applied to psychogenealogy), there is the notion of a big book, much like an accountant's ledger, of familial accounts, listing both debts and assets. The karmic debts are the sums of the accounts (which actually represent our ancestors) that generated debts. But this concept is not about finances. A karmic debt is the trauma and the challenges we struggle to overcome in life. According to the family's legacy, these karmic debts are handed down to descendants and are erased only when resolved. Karmic debts can be very rich and positive or limiting and negative. When a karmic debt is overcome (through symbolic actions, for example), you reap all its positive forces.

KABBALAH

The Kabbalah (הלבק in Hebrew, meaning "reception") is a Jewish esoteric tradition, introduced as "the secret and oral law." It was given to Moses by YHWH (Yahve, the God of Israel). The Kabbalah is made up of complex interactions demonstrating the profound symbolism of numbers. We owe it to two different methods. The first is theosophical reduction, which consists of reducing a two-digit number into one single-digit number (from 1 to 9). For example, $32 = 3 + 2 = 5$. The second method is theosophical addition. It consists in adding up all the numbers from 1 to the chosen number. For example, for number 3: $1 + 2 + 3 = 6$. This method reveals the secret value of a number.

LIFE PATH

Your life path details your personal initiatory road: its purpose, its environment, its climate, and its events. This calculation, based on your date of birth, helps you decipher your personality. It also helps you understand how to accomplish your goals in all the domains of your life by developing your resources and your qualities without ignoring your flaws and limitations. Thanks to the life path, you can more easily determine your life's mission, your purpose, and the most fulfilling direction to take. This is all determined at birth—your deep-rooted personality will be there until the end.

LIFE MISSIONS

Very different from life path (see above), life missions are the possibilities, roles, and projects that are offered to us during our journey, so we can see it through. These missions are tools to help us serve our life path's purpose. To put it concretely, I am currently on a life path ruled by 11 (ambitious realizations, creativity, confidence, surpassing oneself, and inspiration). To complete this path, one of my missions

is to write books, and another is to create oracle and tarot decks. And yet, a lot of people immediately assume that my life path is ruled by 7, because this sacred number favors brainpower, analysis, knowledge of the self, and spirituality.

MASTER NUMBER

A master number is more "powerful" than other numbers because its energetic resource is greater. Master numbers are 11, 22, 33, and more rarely 44 and 55. Because of their repetition, their ability to shine but also to collapse is greater than with "classical" numbers (numbers from 1 to 9).

NUMEROLOGY

Numerology is one of mankind's oldest sciences. Nowadays it's a powerful tool of self-development and growth. Thanks to this accessible technique, we can concretely act on the present, the here and now, and thus create for ourselves a more harmonious, balanced, and fulfilling near future.

Numerical symbolism could predate astrology (planets, zodiac signs) and the tarot. Primitive numbers are pioneers, preceding even writing and language. They were represented by barcodes (composed of notches and stripes) and used to transmit information. It was not until the 11th century that Arabic numbers as we know them were approved.

Some practitioners associate numerology with the first appearances of the Kabbalah in the Bible's Old Testament (see Kabbalah).

NICKNAME (OR PSEUDONYM)

Whether it is a simple name or something associated with a family name, I suggest you study nicknames and pseudonyms of artists and authors. Even if a public persona is sometimes representative of only an infinitesimal part of the private, it is still interesting to identify its impacts and influences.

PYTHAGOREAN ALPHABET

This is a simple technique that rests on the idea that names, family names, and words in general (such as an address, company name, title of a project) have an effect on the energy, personality, and, in some way, destiny of a person. Currently, in this method, the letters of the modern Latin alphabet are assigned numerical values from 1 through 9. This method is also called the Tripoli alphabet, for it was formally recognized by Septimus Tripoli in 1350. This alphabet has been used by shamans for millennia. This simple method is accessible to everyone.

REDUCTION

In numerology, the main mathematical equation used is theosophical addition $(1 + 2 + 9 = 12)$. Please note that a reduction is necessary, and that you must reduce the number you find to get a classical number (from 1 to 9) or a master number (11, 22, 33, 44,

or 55). For the theosophical reduction, we use reduction. For example:
$$1 + 2 + 9 = 12 = 1 + 2 = 3$$

Z

ZERO

Zero is a number that often doesn't exist in most numerological currents. And yet I think the zero is full of meaning.

It represents endless, self-regenerating potential, because it encompasses all that exists. I often compare zero to the color black, which regroups all other colors. I also agree with the author Dan Millman, who says that the zero represents inner gifts.

According to the Kabbalah, zero symbolizes the end of a cycle, since it starts with the letter z. The o represents a new egg, the opening to a new cycle, a fresh start. Zero's anagram is eroz, which can be easily transformed into Eros, the Greek god of creation and love.

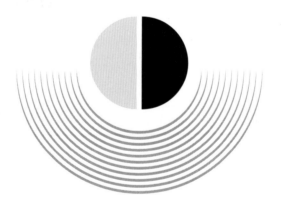

PSEUDONYMS THAT SPEAK VOLUMES Many numerology practitioners don't see the point in looking into pseudonyms and nicknames—and yet they reveal a multitude of relevant information. My personal experience is proof of that.

Throughout my twenties to my thirties, I worked under completely fabricated names for personal and professional reasons. Never doing things halfway, I legally changed my name to the pseudonym I used as a writer and put on my ID. When I discovered numerology, I wanted to do an analysis of myself during this period of my life. Following my tutor's advice, I opted to do this by studying each of my two different names.

I started with my birth name, family name, and date of birth. Then I did a second with my pseudonym, even though I had stopped using it a year prior, as well as my date of birth. And even though my life path was the same in both instances, I can assure you that all my other results were vastly different. Both numerological analyses were correct— and both were very enlightening. Through this persona I had created, I exploited new qualities in myself, developed new talents, and—most importantly—discovered many weaknesses and flaws that revealed my darkest side. In the end, my pseudonym interfered with my personality.

I could have kept this pseudonym for my professional activities. But after a long period of introspection, I decided to go down a more genuine path, a path that was more consistent with the person I really was. It was at this time that I was interviewed by two famous French radio stations, and it became essential to use my birth name. Without fully realizing it at the time, I rejected all the energy and characteristics that belonged to the persona I had created. And you know what? I have never been happier and more fulfilled in the media than at that moment.

THE DIFFERENT NUMEROLOGICAL METHODS

✦

In order to enlighten your first steps through the mysterious world of numbers, it is important to distinguish the different existing numerology methods. I will explain below the eight methods that have most often crossed my path. The interpretations and names I will employ are often personal and contradictory. The common denominator for all these methods is their willingness to reveal, each in their own way, what lies behind the numbers. For that, they use three elements: the name, the family name (birth name or married name for women), and the date of birth. This list is not exhaustive and is only meant to inform.

Pythagorean Numerology

Also called the classical, primary, traditional, or occidental, Pythagorean numerology is the most common method of employing numerology. Created by Pythagoras, it has followed the principles of gematria since antiquity. Gematria is a process that associates a number with a word, for which we add together the numerical and symbolic values of each letter (see the Pythagorean alphabet in the lexicon on p. 29). In Pythagorean numerology, we use numbers from 1 to 9. Some practitioners sometimes don't reduce the master numbers (11, 22, 33, 44, and 55), but it's rarer.

Kabbalistic Numerology

This calculation method is derived from the Kabbalah and based on the Hebraic alphabet (see Kabbalah, p. 27). It is made up of twenty-two numbers

THE LIMITS OF PYTHAGOREAN NUMEROLOGY
This method can only be applied to the letters in alphabets like the Arabic, Latin, or Cyrillic alphabet. It cannot be applied to pictorial or expression-based alphabets like hieroglyphics, Japanese kanji, or Chinese characters.

(from 1 to 400), following the numeric attribution of the Sephiroth (the ten creative powers of the Kabbalah in its mystical approach). The kabbalistic method relies on various hermeneutic techniques (the interpretation of signs as the symbolic elements of a culture) including gematria, much like Pythagorean numerology. Moreover, kabbalistic numerology practitioners see numbers as living beings. Just like with classical numerology, they mostly use the theosophical addition and reduction (see Reduction, p. 29) for their equations.

Karmic Numerology

This method derives from kabbalistic numerology. Based on the association of karma with numbers and their powers, the concept of reincarnation and multiple lives is at the core of this system. For this numerology's practitioners, karma is made up of life lessons to learn, challenges to overcome, and life missions to complete in all of our earthly incarnations. If our choices are harmful and move us toward failure, we must repay this karmic debt in our next life.

Karmic numbers (also called missing numbers) are grouped in a table or grid but are also hidden behind the numbers of all names, family names, and even our date of birth. Thus, all the people born during the 20th century, in 1900 or later, will wear the karmic debt 19 (see p. 27). This karmic debt is attached to the memory of abuse of authority and power. This debt expresses a general conflict, a confrontation with authority and hierarchy, or, on the other hand, with submission, sacrifice, or one's own power.

Note that karmic debts 13, 14, 15, 16, 19, 26, and 33 cannot be reduced, for they all correspond to a specific transgenerational memory.

Chinese Numerology

Chinese numerology doesn't have an exact date of creation. It is indeed hard to determine when it was really discovered. Some numerology practitioners say that its creation dates back to when Emperor Wu saw a turtle with nine scales on its back. This gave him the idea to use a nine-square grid for numerology. This grid would later be called Lo Shu (洛书), which literally means "the book of the River Luo." The sum of the numbers that compose it always equals fifteen, whether you add them up horizontally, vertically, or diagonally.

4	9	2
3	5	7
8	1	6

The importance of this number is influenced by astrology. It takes the moon exactly fifteen days to cycle from the new moon to the full moon. Some Chinese practitioners affirm that Chinese numerology, much like Chinese astrology, started at the same time as the

Chinese calendar, more than five thousand years ago.

The Numerology of Ailexin

The numerology of Ailexin is based on tantric numerology, which is itself based on the Sanskrit alphabet. This method offers a deep analysis of the consultant's date of birth. The day corresponds to the soul, the month to the personality, and the last numbers of the year to the consultant's main gift. The year of birth in its entirety reveals the past life. The consultant's life mission is the sum of their day, month, and year of birth. Ailexin uses numbers up to 11.

Chaldean Numerology

Also called mystic or psychic numerology, Chaldean numerology is based on ancient Babylonian tradition. It's one of the oldest methods we know of. It integrates astrology, which greatly influences the interpretation of numbers from 1 to 8. A letter of the alphabet is attributed to each number from 1 to 8. The number 9 is not a part of this method, because it is seen as a sacred number. It is the same for double-digit numbers, which are seen as mighty and powerful. In Chaldean numerology, the calculation's results are not reduced. Double-digit numbers must remain as such. Single-digit numbers (1 to 9) reflect the external aspect of a personality, while same-digit double-digit

numbers (11, 22, 33, and 44) reveal its internal aspect.

Humanist Numerology

Also called psychonumerology, humanist numerology is a modern method. It deciphers unconscious family commitments. It aims to free one from reductive patterns of replication in psychogenealogy.

Indian Numerology

Also known as Tamoul or Tamil numerology, Indian numerology is based upon the calculation of three principal numbers. These numbers are the psychic number, the destiny number, and the name number.

In addition to these eight main methods, you will find strategic and tantric numerology; numerology applied to psychogenealogy; as well as Mayan, evolutive, sacred, astrological, animal, timeless, Sufi, creative, Vedic, celestial, and vibratory numerology; numerology through tarot; and even geonumerology.

All these methods perfectly show the diversity and richness of different techniques. None of them is better than the other, and some even complete and enrich each other. If you are inexperienced, I believe it's essential to begin with the basics of the Pythagorean method. I base my practice of rational and intuitive numerology upon this method.

NUMEROLOGY THROUGHOUT HISTORY

✦

For the sake of transparency, I want to immediately unveil the mysteries of the history of numerology. I would be lying if I assured you that we now perfectly know its origins and history. They actually haven't been fully established yet. However, what is certain is that human beings have always wanted to understand their environment, origins, and roots in order to explain the meaning and reasons for their existence. To satisfy this legitimate curiosity, humans quickly started to create tangible and rational concepts.

A FEW IMPORTANT DATES

More Than 10,000 Years Ago: Origins

Ten-thousand-year-old writing has been discovered, but numerology is probably much older than that. Numerical symbolism predates astrology and tarot, not to mention written communication and language.

Around 480 BCE: The Golden Ratio

This date marks the birth of phi, the perfect number, more commonly called the golden ratio. It is supposedly named phi in honor of Phidias, the ancient Greek sculptor who saw a divine dimension and perfect proportions within this number. This universal number is thought to contain the secret code to each creation of the Universe. According to other theories, numerology is based upon it.

Around 460 BCE: Pythagoras

The different numerological methods seem to be partially connected to Pythagoras's theories. The famous philosopher and mathematician, who lived from 580 to 495 BCE, is regarded as the father of numerology. His theories proved that everything that exists is a number. Following this idea, the Universe is controlled by numbers.

From 430 to 350 BCE: The Reflection

Numerology stirs up the curiosity of many philosophers, like Plato or Socrates. They then try to decipher the nature around them by using the mathematical language.

2nd through 5th Centuries CE: Religion

Saint Ambrose, Saint Clement of Alexandria, and Saint Augustine were all inspired by Pythagorean theories to decipher some parts of the Bible from a numerological perspective. Later, during the Middle Ages, this method was used by the Church to interpret sacred texts.

12th Century: The Endorsement

Arabic numerals as we know them today weren't widely used before the 12th century. In everyday life, these numbers give us a stable point of reference, a safe setting. They help us split and limit not only space, time, distances, and weight, but also people. From calendars (day, weeks, months, years) to seasons (winter, spring, summer, fall) and more general time cycles (based on the rotation of Earth every twenty-four hours), every culture has created a basic calculation for understanding their world, which has been beneficial to their evolution and expansion. Numbers are considered universal symbols, and we can find them in every tradition. Everyone has their own theories about their symbolism, meaning, frame of reference, and use. Numerology easily transforms over time, influenced by cultural interpretations.

17th Century: Astronomy

Mathematicians, physicians, and astronomers Galileo and Johannes Kepler incorporate numerology into their work. According to Kepler, the layouts of some astrological angles are directly connected to numbers.

18th Century: The Age of Enlightenment

The philosophy of Pythagoras was already in vogue during the Enlightenment. It inspired intellectuals like Denis Diderot.

From the 19th Century Onward: Success

More and more intellectuals take an interest in numerology: Honoré de Balzac, Gustave Flaubert, Albert Einstein, Sigmund Freud, and Max Planck were all interested in numerology. History even tells us that a Benedictine monk used it to reveal the outcome of some battles to Napoleon Bonaparte.

> **MYSTERIOUS ORIGINS**
> Many numerologists maintain that the method used at this time originated in China (with the Yi-King, a divination tool), Japan, India, Mesopotamia, Great Britain, and even Egypt— well before the Greeks and Romans became aware of it.

IMPORTANT FEMALE FIGURES After World War I, astrology stole the limelight from numerology. Its modern form, which took shape at the beginning of the 20th century, helped rekindle interest in the United States. Its revival was inspired by the work of Sarah L. Dow Balliett, who wrote many books about numerology from 1905 to 1922. It's believed that her friend, Julia Seton Sears, helped her come up with the name *numerology* during this period.

In 1931, another woman, Florence Campbell, wrote the book *Your Days Are Numbered*. This book would become a big part in the development of contemporary numerology, becoming known in subsequent decades as a solid reference that many other numerologists relied upon as they continued to innovate and popularize this practice.

The research of these visionary women led them to ally their knowledge of numbers' vibrations with wide-scale data analysis. The connection between a person and the numbers that belonged to them was born.

2

NUMEROLOGY
AND YOU

IN THIS SECOND chapter, I'm inviting you to question your-self about your relationship to numerology. Is it symbiotic, cordial, or a love/hate relationship? Test yourself to find out! Then I will share some easy advice to help you find balance.

Moreover, shaking up common misconceptions about numerology will help you discover what beliefs and challenges could get in the way between you and the third and fourth chapters. Those last two chapters will allow you to practice numerology with both of your brain's hemispheres.

YOUR RELATIONSHIP
TO NUMEROLOGY

✦

Is it really the right time for you to practice numerology? Are you open and available enough? I'm inviting you to take the following tests to confirm that this is an enthusiastic yes or to help you turn this into the ideal moment.

TEST YOURSELF!

Take a deep breath and calmly read the following affirmations. In complete honesty and transparency with yourself, select the sentences that apply to you. Calculate the total for each question, sum them up, and discover your result. Let's go!

Question 1: Who I Am

☐ I am an open-minded person who easily accepts different points of view than mine.
☐ People say I'm a bit kooky and mystical.
☐ I'm a particularly curious person.
☐ I'm a born searcher; I love to explore, rummage through, and go into things in depth to better understand them.
☐ I am not trying to believe and live according to one single truth.
☐ I am eager to learn and don't expect people to tell me what I want to hear.
☐ I understand that things aren't black or white (people, numbers . . .).
☐ I am open to discovery and novelty.
☐ I am aware that I possess great flaws, formidable qualities, and a precious inner power.
☐ Whenever I want to, I easily let go of things, and I feel psychologically stable.

TOTAL 1 = ...

Question 2: What I Like

☐ I prefer simple calculations that quickly lead to a precise result.
☐ I prefer practical self-development methods (like life or professional coaching) over long-time support (like psychoanalysis).
☐ I like to make connections and associations between different themes and fields.
☐ I believe that life is so rich that it deserves to be perpetually explored.
☐ I am passionate about self-development (books, workshops, training courses, initiations . . .).
☐ I love answering tests like this.
☐ I believe in the power of words and numbers.
☐ I want to learn new methods to better know and surpass myself so I can evolve.
☐ I don't believe in equality but in equity, for there are different gifts lying dormant withing us, all waiting to be awoken.
☐ I like to immediately put in practice what I learn.

TOTAL 2 = ...

TOTAL 1 + 2 = ...

RESULTS

If you have selected 16 or more affirmations, the answer to the question "Is it really the right time to use numerology?" is "Yes!" Congratulations! This is the ideal moment for you. Since you possess all the skills you will need in the two final chapters of this book, you should take great pleasure in practicing numerology with both of your brain's hemispheres. Nevertheless, I invite you to assimilate all the moments of rational and intuitive numerology step by step. The assimilation should be done in tune with your rhythm. To preserve your beautiful personal balance, look at my recommendations below.

If you have selected from 8 to 15 affirmations, well done, especially if the totals for each of the two questions are similar. If that's not the case yet, maximize your assets with my recommendations. This will help you open yourself to the beautiful relationship to numbers that awaits you.

If you have selected 7 affirmations or fewer, I invite you to deeply question yourself, without any judgment. On a scale of 0 to 10, how are you feeling right now? If curiosity and joy are still motivating you, don't give up. Remind yourself of the reasons that pushed you to open this book. Why is it important to you to discover rational and intuitive numerology? To reach your goal, take action by trying out my suggestions below. Take the time to assimilate them and respect your rhythm.

MY ADVICE TO BALANCE OUT
YOUR RELATIONSHIP WITH NUMBERS

Cultivate an Open Mind

By nature, humans aren't attracted to things that differ from their frame of reference. Open-mindedness is thus not intuitive. A rigid education and the handing down of unconscious fears lead to closed-up children who will, in turn, become closed-minded adults. I could stop here, on a very negative note, but you know what? There is plenty of positive in all this, because everything in life can be transformed and transfigured if you really want to. The secret is to do it step by step and respect your inner rhythm. To reach the top of the mountain, you must do it one step at a time. It's the same thing with open-mindedness. Begin by attentively listening to speeches and stances, and by observing different behaviors than yours. By doing this, you will seize many opportunities to learn and explore novelty. If you quickly fall back into judgmental behaviors, replace your preconceptions and limiting beliefs by asking open-ended questions in order to learn more. Behind every attitude, behind all sentences and words, there is a hidden reason that deserves to exist even if you don't understand it.

Develop Your Curiosity

Even if we don't all possess the same potential, every human is born curious. Remember when you were a child. I am sure that you were eager to learn anything that could help you know more about others and the world around you. When we're young, we generally want to understand, see, try, and experiment with everything. As the years go by, this enthusiasm falters and sometimes completely disappears.

Become Aware of Your Own Worth

This advice is particularly directed at you if you haven't selected the affirmation "I am aware that I possess great flaws, formidable qualities, and a precious inner power." The philosopher and poet Ralph Waldo Emerson wrote: "Self-trust is the first secret of success."

The word esteem comes from the French word estimer, which itself comes from the Latin word *aestimare*, which means "to value." In

French, *estimer* means to "determine something's worth" but also "to have an opinion about something." And so self-esteem is in fact two opinions: the one you have about yourself and the one other have about you.

Self-esteem is about the positive evaluation of yourself, based on how aware you are of your own worth. It is essential to everyone. People with high self-esteem will treat themselves and others with kindness. They feel worthy of love.

The three pillars of self-esteem are self-love, a good image of what you represent, and having trust in what you accomplish. Do you believe that the more you accomplish in life, the more you increase your ability to achieve things?

I suggest that you implement a few small habits to nourish one or more pillars of your self-esteem. For instance, treat yourself by surrounding yourself with positive and kind people, or by taking five minutes of your day to enjoy a soothing beverage or to call a friend. If you place yourself at the center of your life again, if you take care of yourself, you will take back your personal power.

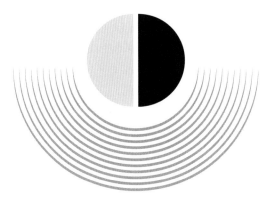

NO MORE LIMITING BELIEFS OR MISCONCEPTIONS

✦

FOUR COMMON MISCONCEPTIONS

ABOUT NUMEROLOGY

Here are four common misconceptions some of my consultants have shared with me in the past. Some may seem too rough to be true, and yet I have heard them before.

Misconception 1

Numerology Is Extraordinary and Limitless

FALSE. According to their feedback, my clients find my interpretations to be 90 percent accurate. And yet I always keep in mind that numerology and human beings are limited. These limitations can be helpful (positive) or restrictive (negative). Our environment, family, culture, traditions, and beliefs and the many choices we make are all important factors. They influence and stimulate our personality, belief system, and behavior and all the aspects of our lives. Nothing is set in stone. Everything is in a state of constant metamorphosis. Every minute we live give us endless possibilities of countless choices.

In numerology, there is no determinism, no certitude, no inevitability,

and no absolute truth. We cannot discover everything, learn everything, or pass down everything. This method isn't really an end it itself. It is a tool for self-development. I provide information to all my consultants; I do not impose declarations upon them. When practicing numerology, it is essential to remind ourselves that nothing is frozen in time. Everything is transformed. Everything changes.

Misconception 2

I've Been Told Some Numbers Are Better Than Others

FALSE. No number is better, more powerful, or more advantageous than another. It's true that that a master number (11, 22, 33, 44, or 55) possesses a greater energy resource than a basic number (1 to 9). Number 44, for instance, is double the power of the number 4 and also amplifies the energy of the number 8 (because $4 + 4 = 8$). But beware: the other side of the coin is just as great for the master number. Thus, an 11 that doesn't channel their creative energy and their gifts (mediumship, divination, healing, helping others) is more likely to develop patterns of addiction or irrational, excessive, and disproportionate behaviors. Doesn't sound so glamorous all of sudden, does it?

Misconception 3

Astrology, Divination, and Numerology Are the Same Thing

FALSE. Astrology is the art of determining someone's personality and destiny through the study and interpretation of the stars. Numerology probably predates astrology, since primitive numbers predate writing and language. Numerology doesn't need any planet, celestial pattern, or zodiac signs, only numbers. The clairvoyants' psychic abilities to "see clearly" the past, present, and future has no correlation to numerology. You can practice numerology without communicating with the dead, remembering your dreams, or having prophetic dreams.

Misconception 4

You Need to Possess a Gift to Practice Numerology

FALSE. I've read and heard before that I had an exceptional gift. My ego is happy to know that, but I immediately stop the consultants who tell me that, because it's simply not true! Indeed, numerology is absolutely not about possessing some sort of gift. It's a specific method you apply. The only things that can differentiate numerologists are going to be speed, the accuracy of an analysis, and the extent of their knowledge. This can be learned by anyone! Anyone can be interested in numerology and practice it. Some might just more easily understand logical interpretations (through rational numerology) or symbolic interpretations (thought intuitive numerology), while others might need to work harder for it.

NUMEROLOGY AND THE LEFT BRAIN

✦

THE STAR OF this third chapter is the left hemisphere of your brain. Logic, rationality, organization, analytical processing, calculation—so many abilities are deeply connected to your left brain. A little reminder: rational numerology is inseparable from this hemisphere. Thus, to feed it and discover the traditional aspect of numerology, I am inviting you to explore identity calculations, enlightened calculations, and life calculations.

PRELIMINARY CALCULATIONS

✦

Before you can start calculating, it's important to apply the Pythagorean alphabet (see p. 29) to your names in order to change the letters of your name and surname into numbers (from 1 to 9).

1	2	3	4	5	6	7	8	9
A	B	C	D	E	F	G	H	I
J	K	L	M	N	O	P	Q	
S	T	U	V	W	X	Y	Z	R

Use your customary first name and any other first name in your personal records. Treat a hyphenated first name as one name, for it is a whole. For instance, the name Anne-Sophie is only one name.

If you have changed personal information as a child (if you were adopted, acknowledged as someone's child, or otherwise changed your name), trust this information and not your birth personal records.

If these changes happened as an adult (like a woman taking her husband's name after a wedding), the influence of this name on your personality and traits will only be effective once you'll have lived as much time with this new name as you did with the old one. For example, if you got married at 25, your married name will only replace your maiden name when you turn 50.

For nicknames and professional aliases, see pages 29 and 31.

My Preliminary Calculations
This is a fictitious example (for I have other names and surnames):
V = vowels (A, E, I, O, U, Y)
C = consonants (all other letters)
Differentiating vowels from consonants will come in handy for some calculations.

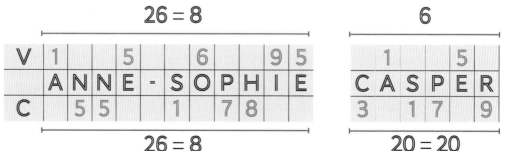

50

IDENTITY CALCULATIONS

These basic calculations only affect your identity: your first name and surname. Since no number is only positive or negative, each result is made of two parts: the strengths (the positive aspect) and the challenges (the negative aspect). With this information, I invite you to fill in the numbers on the following pages. For each calculation below, reduce the result number into a number from 1 to 9. Only master numbers 11, 22, and 33 shouldn't be reduced.

THE ACTIVE NUMBER

This is the total of the vowels and consonants of your customary first name only.

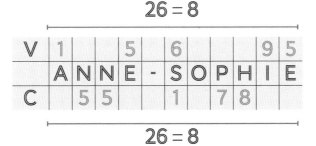

For Anne-Sophie Casper, we only use "Anne-Sophie":

$$1 + 5 + 6 + 9 + 5 + 5 + 5 + 1 + 7 + 8 = 52 = 5 + 2 = 7$$

Write your active number here: _____.

Your customary first name actively influences your behavior and personality. It is the essence of your nature. The active number tells you how you act in everyday life, how you work, and how you interact with people (mostly your collaborators, classmates, and so on). It reveals the tangible ways you use to exteriorize and assert your personality, as well as your own potential.

IF YOU GET THE NUMBER:

Your personality is strong and authoritarian

Strengths: desire for success, great at decision-making, efficiency, innovation, willpower, initiative, active and dynamic disposition, ambition, independence, passion, bravery, great power, enthusiasm, and inventiveness.

Challenges: frank and direct personality, intimidation, selfishness, demanding nature, impatience, nervousness, opportunism, manipulation, cold demeanor, intolerance, lack of discipline, great need for recognition and self-expression, and lack of attentiveness and open-mindedness.

Your nature is soft and naïve

Strengths: sensitive and reassuring personality, generosity, patience, diplomacy, selflessness, adaptability, kindness, calmness, sharing, active listening, humility, mediation, interpersonal skills, and human contact.

Challenges: ingenuous and fragile nature, anxiety, hypocrisy, inconsistency, apathy, bad stress and emotional management, oversensitivity, fear of conflict, extreme devotion, impossibility to be on your own, and great affective needs to fill.

Your personality is original and fickle

Strengths: atypical personality, great imagination, sociability, extroversion, communication skills, interpersonal skills, creativity, sharing, dexterity, nonconforming, balance, open-mindedness, intelligence, optimism, and enthusiasm.

Challenges: erratic nature, dispersion, manipulation through seduction, impatience, struggles with money management, pride, indifference, anger, resentment, jealousy, craving praise and recognition, recklessness, shallowness, intrusion, and great need to be admired.

Your nature is straight and inflexible

Strengths: trustworthy and forthright personality, power, insight, patience, realization, sense of duty and responsibility, rigor, respect, work, construction, efficient organization, accomplishment, sincerity, bravery, prudence, discipline, demanding nature, and perseverance.

Challenges: harsh nature, extreme rectitude, authoritarianism, being stuck in a routine, greed, too controlling with yourself and others, insensitivity, afraid to step out of your comfort zone, rational mind, closed-mindedness, lack of whimsy, and casualness.

Your personality is dynamic and erratic

Strengths: flexible personality, sharp-mindedness, mobility, constant replenishment, adaptability, novelty, charm, enthusiasm, humor, and boldness.

Challenges: fickle nature, dispersion, impulsivity, impatience, lack of discipline, extreme independence, strong taste for danger and change, infidelity, constant need for new experiences, and fear of routines.

Your nature is responsible and shy

Strengths: balances personality, sincerity, calmness, ability to keep and honor engagements, adaptability, intelligence, endurance, softness, willpower, sensitivity, human warmth, consistency, creativity, and intuition.

Challenges: impressionable nature, indecisiveness, instability, dependent nature, excessive search for aesthetics, oversensitivity, extreme reaction to injustice, demanding, cold and insensitive demeanor, sarcasm, and guilt-tripping.

Your personality is independent and solitary

Strengths: calm personality; sincerity; active listening; great at giving advice; ability to analyze, synthesize, and reflect; open-mindedness; good understanding of others and yourself; and talent for introspection.

Challenges: selfish nature, difficulty to trust others, solitude, passive behavior, melancholy, second-guessing one's decisions, anxiety, doubt, zealotry, mysterious, stubbornness, perfectionism, extreme prudence, and inability to change your mind.

Your nature is energetic and impulsive

Strengths: active personality, benevolence, power, honesty, determination, construction, ability to accomplish things, generosity, loyalty, stability, courage, combativeness, charisma, presence, and assertiveness.

Challenges: bad temper, tendencies to hold grudges, demanding nature, inflexibility, stubbornness, excessive nature, possessiveness, constant struggle to stay on top, authoritarian attitude, control freak, fear of losing, extreme focus on performance, insensitivity, and domineering attitude.

Your personality is selfless and emotional

Strengths: passionate personality, generosity, open-mindedness, loyalty, benevolence, empathy, compassion, optimism, orderly nature, consistency, stability, devotion, seriousness, good-natured personality, and energy put in service of a greater good.

Challenges: overly demanding nature, daydreaming, extreme perfectionism, bad self-esteem, naïveté, melancholy, dishonesty, fear of romanticism, sadness, lack of practicality, untidiness, and depression.

Your nature is inspired and nervous

Strengths: inspiring personality, great intuition, strength, tenacity, willpower, self-control, spiritual and psychic power, great intellect, truthful, diligent worker, discretion, unusual moral strength, and great inner richness.

Challenges: authoritarian nature, extreme sensitivity, workaholism, disharmony, overly intense energy, strong taste for luxury, perfectionism, high ideals, frustration, superiority complex, self-importance, egocentricity, lack of openness toward others, and stubbornness.

Your personality is inspiring and stubborn

Strengths: inspired personality, great ability to turn creative inspiration into tangible creations, humanitarian mission, courage, resistance, high expectations, surpassing yourself, and infectious energy.

Challenges: insatiable nature, materialistic, instability, nervousness, extreme tension, depression, frustration, self-destruction, provocation, overzealousness, egocentricity, pride, and stubbornness.

Your nature is rare and demanding

Strengths: pure personality, seriousness, discipline, curiosity, deep and powerful inner thoughts, strength, imagination, sharp-mindedness, attractiveness, unconditional love, and efficient and sincere communication.

Challenges: very controlling nature, strong authoritarianism, individualism, deep instability, nervousness, extreme self-sacrifice, and intense emotional turmoil.

THE HEREDITARY NUMBER

The hereditary number is the sum of the vowels and consonants of the family name only.

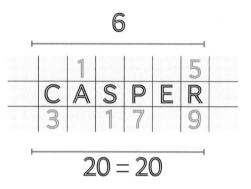

For Anne-Sophie Casper, you only use Casper:

$$1 + 5 + 3 + 1 + 7 + 9 = 26 = 2 + 6 = 8$$

Write your hereditary number here: _____

The hereditary number corresponds to all the things that have been passed down by your family name, the family's heredity. It usually applies to your father's lineage, if he gave you his name. It includes all the values and family principles bequeathed to you.

Know that what you have inherited from your family name is not necessarily what you will keep or what you will develop in your life. You can take it all, or reject it all, or keep only a part of it.

Still, it is what has been given to you through the passing down of your family name.

IF YOU GET THE NUMBER:

You are from a brave and opportunistic family
Strengths: strong-willed personality, great self-confidence, powerful energy, strength, ambition, assertiveness, fast learner, resourcefulness, intelligence, and business-minded.

Challenges: profiteering nature, deep need to assert yourself, aggressiveness, pride, closed-mindedness, impatience, individualism, selfishness, overindulgence, and emotional excesses.

In your family, people are sociable and emotional
Strengths: open and stable personality, tolerance, respect, empathy, comprehension, collaboration, sharing, manners, softness, tenderness, calmness, discretion, safety, warmth, mediation, and being loving toward others.

Challenges: fragile nature, devotion to the extreme, oversensitive, indecisiveness, doubt, passiveness, victimization, fear, anxiety, poor stress management, and tendency to overlook and sacrifice yourself.

You are from an ambitious and rebellious family
Strengths: artistic personality, passion, adaptability, sociability, intelligence, originality, inventiveness, creativity, self-control, open-mindedness, dexterity, humor, sense of adventure, novelty, charm, and seduction.

Challenges: critical nature, great need for focus and guidance, deep fear of loneliness, scattered mind, nonchalance, shallowness, lack of self-confidence, restlessness, and overwhelming need for novelty.

In your family, people are reliable and fussy

Strengths: organized and reliable personality, balance, stability, structure, seriousness, rectitude, sincerity, methodology, pragmatism, being in touch with reality, dignified attitude, analytical skills, good work ethic, and ability to understand and interpret.

Challenges: inflexible nature, lack of fantasy and humor, closed-mindedness, authoritarianism, extreme discipline, lack of imagination and creativity, fear of the future, and difficulty in doing "useless" things.

You are from a free-spirited family in need of guidance

Strengths: flexible and combative personality, mobility, courage, bravery, determination, curiosity, fervor, sense of adventure, discoveries, a taste for challenges and new experiences, and intelligent and responsive mind.

Challenges: unstable nature that is sometimes hard to follow, scattered mind, loose morals, brazenness, boastfulness, pride, selfishness, lack of balance, stubbornness, inconsistence, and frivolity.

In your family, people are congenial and indecisive

Strengths: generous personality, honesty, sincerity, honesty, sharing, benevolence, goodness, loyalty, sense of family, practicality, rightfulness, demanding nature, fidelity, warmth, reliability, and responsibility.

Challenges: jealous nature, intrusive, unstable, gossips, hypocrisy, resentment, oversensitivity, uncertainty, doubt, being overly protective, and affective and emotional struggles.

You are from an accepting and elusive family

Strengths: realistic and reasoned personality, independence, autonomy, astute psychology, wisdom, calmness, diligence, goodness, sense of justice, truthfulness, spirituality, analytical skills, ability to reflect on the world, intelligence, rich and intense inner world.

Challenges: distant nature, aloofness, solitude, being closed off, withdrawal, being overly perfectionist, being too controlling, being overly invested in every aspect of your life, melancholy, self-doubt, anxiety and doubt.

In your family, people are active and domineering

Strengths: determined personality, courage, sense of justice, ability to overcome obstacles, creativity, inventiveness, novelty, passion, strength, ambition, boldness, independence, perseverance, competitiveness, negotiation, commitment, and hard work.

Challenges: stubborn and resolute nature, impulsiveness, aggressiveness, authoritarianism, influence, power, being commanding, recklessness, obstinacy, being uncompromising, nervousness, selfishness, intolerance, and being too controlling of yourself and others.

You are from a generous and proud family

Strengths: altruistic personality, sensitivity, humanitarianism, open-mindedness, having an open heart, tolerance, compassion, freedom, independence, growth, a passion for traveling, discovery, and ability to easily open yourself to others and the world.

Challenges: egotistical nature, self-love, paranoia, being overly emotional, inconstance, extreme self-sacrifice, overly high ideals, individualism, and dissatisfaction caused by an incessant quest for something better.

In your family, people are magnetic and anxious

Strengths: ambitious personality, sense of human values, self-control, strength, courage, determination, good intuition, helpful, sharing, collaborating, great willpower, inspiration, and persuasive.

Challenges: nervous nature, inner struggle, brutality, impatience, perfectionism, excess of energy, authoritarianism, and poor stress management.

You are from an enterprising and impatient family

Strengths: responsible personality, high expectations, great aspirations, inspiration, fervor, determination, realization, being enterprising and taking initiative, intuition, ambitious projects.

Challenges: tenacious and stubborn nature, nervousness, frustration, dissatisfaction, obsessiveness, perfectionism, extravagance, illusion, and overworking yourself.

In your family, people are loyal and accommodating

Strengths: rare and extremely powerful personality, universal love, great generosity, natural ability to comfort and welcome others as they are, accuracy, demanding nature, loyalty, reliability, sincerity, and sense of family and community.

Challenges: devoted nature, self-sacrifice and forgetting about your own needs, indecisiveness, bad self-esteem, oversensitivity, uncertainty, doubt, and extreme protectiveness.

THE EXPRESSION NUMBER

The expression number is the sum of the vowels and consonants of all the surnames and the family name.

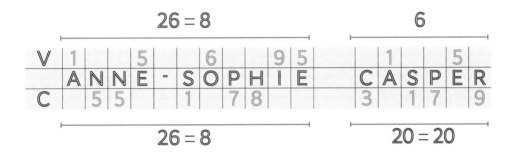

For Anne-Sophie Casper, we use the whole:

$$1 + 5 + 6 + 9 + 5 + 1 + 5 + 5 + 5 + 1 + 7 + 8 + 3 + 1 + 7 + 9 = 78$$
$$= 7 + 8 = 15 = 1 + 5 = 6$$

Write your expression number here: _____

The expression number designates all the main elements of your nature and behavior. It's the summary of your profound motivation and personality. This number represents the psychological profile of each person. It's your personality as it appears to others.

The expression number is also linked to your profession, what others can guess about you, and what you're willing to show the world. This number is very important: it individualizes you and greatly influences your life missions.

IF YOU GET THE NUMBER:

You are an independent and ambitious person

Strengths: creative sense, determination, communication, solar energy, self-made realization, energy, innovation, being at the center of the action, driven creative talent, good organizational skills, and decision-making.

Challenges: selfishness; individualism; egocentricity; nervousness; impulsiveness; domineering personality; feelings of rejection; authority; leadership; victimization; intolerance; tyranny; aggressivity; stubbornness; struggles with accepting hierarchy, rules, and boundaries; and executive mismanagement.

You are a diplomatic and patient person

Strengths: good at helping people and helping other people grow, good second in command, active listening, softness, affection, sensitivity, sharing, and a need for shared realization with others.

Challenges: moody nature, follower, passiveness, lack of self-esteem, oversensitivity, withdrawal, fears of being incompetent, indifference, self-limitations (physical, mental, emotional), panic, isolation, anxiety, and feelings of inadequacy.

You are an extroverted artist

Strengths: creativity, enthusiasm, interpersonal skills, acute sense of equity, artistic expression, novelty, great at connecting with others, natural ability to express yourself and communicate, joy, sociability, sharp-mindedness, and great capacity to act.

Challenges: easily offended, impulsiveness, aggressivity, immaturity, naïveté, idle talk, passing fancies, isolation, anger, scattered mind, oversensitivity, vanity, frivolity, superficiality, excessive focus on appearances, being dispersed, and overspending.

You are a hardworking and courageous person

Strengths: perseverance; hardworking; being organized; physical, moral, and emotional resistance; determination; concentration; seriousness; order; consistency; tenacity; and a need to build strong and durable things.

Challenges: lack of humor, closed-mindedness, placid appearance, emotional insecurity, overly worrying, routine, rigidity, irritability, fear, doubt, being too conservative, obsessiveness, poor stress management, and overly rational mind.

You are an audacious and dynamic person

Strengths: being open about every aspect of life (psychologic, emotional, physical), energy, sharp-mindedness, great potential, mobility, independence, adaptation, motion, innovation, great communication, and persuasive.

Challenges: nervousness, versatility, moody and unstable nature, a deep need for variety and changes, mandatory freedom of action, regular mood swings, manipulation, impulsiveness, opportunism, and a visceral fear of feeling confined and imprisoned.

You are an intuitive and loyal person

Strengths: a good sense of responsibility and service; harmony; balance; sharing; active participation in pleasant, healthy, and serene settings; being respectful of your own values; and the ability to guide and coach people.

Challenges: jealousy; envy; irresponsibility; a deep need for harmony; acting as a victim, bully, or manipulator; struggles with decision-making; sentiments over reason; anger; and provocation.

You are an original friend

Strengths: having a sense for sharing, imagination, unusual intelligence, uniqueness, great understanding (of yourself and others), sharp instincts, sharpness of heart and mind, great spirituality, and natural ability to teach and pass down knowledge.

Challenges: pessimism, isolation, secrecy, aloofness, misanthropy, being reserved, hypocrisy, deep lack of self-esteem, pretentiousness, arrogance, introverted and solitary nature, fear of running out of money, deep need of escape, and sarcastic humor people rarely enjoy.

You are a decided creator

Strengths: great reserve of energy, independence, autonomy, determination, positiveness, solid self-esteem, self-confidence, sense of initiative and action, combative nature, willpower, justice, and a need to rise through construction and self-realization.

Challenges: high level of expectations, stubbornness, strong personality, obstinate nature, aggressiveness, impulsivity, dishonesty, fear of inaction, demanding nature, refusal to do things by half, perpetually intense rhythm, and difficulty with taking orders.

You are a committed humanist

Strengths: long-term commitment, great spirituality, open-mindedness, passion, emotions, understanding, good at communication, learning and teaching, respect, inclusive vision, acts of service, and being open to the world.

Challenges: extremism; a need for love (given and received); zealotry; overemotional; nervousness; idealism; high ideals; devotion; oversensitivity; depression; and emotional, psychological, and nervous unbalance.

You are an ambitious and determined person

Strengths: great strength; natural ability to bring out the best in people, ideas, and concepts; great determination; inspiration; being detail oriented; acute intuition; and quick connection between the brain and the heart.

Challenges: oversensitivity, demanding nature, absolutism, perfectionism, authoritarianism, difficulties to channel your energy, egocentricity, doubt, excessive self-questioning, lack of trust and self-confidence, and a constant need to surpass yourself.

You are a productive and ambitious person

Strengths: great aspiration, gentle but solid strength, fervor, balance, responsibility, courage, acute intuition, unusual productivity, and a need to evolve and grow rapidly.

Challenges: lack of balance between personal and work life, workaholic, overworking, individualism, nervousness, selfishness, excessive ambition, self-consciousness, and egocentricity.

You are an altruistic and sensitive person

Strengths: rare and exceptional qualities, sincerity, originality, generosity, goodness, understanding, loyalty, emotional intelligence, reliability, honesty, and being open to the world.

Challenges: misanthropy, able to accomplish both the best and the worst, vulnerability, being easily offended, lack of willpower, fear of failure and abandonment, elusive nature, overemotional, involuntary marginalization, and victimization.

THE ASPIRATION NUMBER

The aspiration number is the sum of all the vowels (surnames and family name).

For Anne-Sophie Casper:

$$1 + 5 + 6 + 9 + 5 + 1 + 5 = 32 = 3 + 2 = 5$$

Write your aspiration number here: _____

The aspiration number is also called the soul urge number and the heart's desire number. It reveals how you must become accomplished in life. It's the number of your private life, the trajectory you must take, especially once you turn thirty-five. The aspiration number signifies the soul's desire, nature, and motivations (conscious and unconscious), but also the unconscious, the description of the self, the mental vibration that enlivens you from within, the heart of your personality, and your most intimate ambitions.

IF YOU GET THE NUMBER:

You enjoy being in charge and making the decisions

Strengths: sensibility, will to succeed, originality, great ability to work, competence, temerity, courage, belief, independence, freedom, autonomy, and an innate talent for accomplishing big projects on your own.

Challenges: selfishness, loneliness, stubbornness, pride, aloofness, aggressiveness, egocentricity, vanity, arrogance, conceit, domination, authoritarianism, intolerance, lack of tact, constant need for validation, and struggles with criticism and authority.

You are a creator of links, a connector

Strengths: ability to create associations and alliances, acts of service, understanding, sociability, loyalty, patience, resourcefulness, reliability, affection, softness, mediation, balance, emotional maturity, and intuition.

Challenges: passiveness, manipulation, fragility, credulity, being too accommodating, influence, victimization, idleness, lack of discipline, lack of ambition, constant self-doubt, loss of identity and guilt-tripping.

You enjoy art and its multiple applications

Strengths: sociability, imagination, simplicity, dexterity, enthusiasm, intuition, harmony, aesthetics, friendship, extroversion, sharp-minded, goodness, politeness, good manners, creativity, great potential.

Challenges: lack of balance, vanity, criticism, misplaced pride, lack of seriousness, charlatanism, shallowness, showing off, scattered mind, oversensitivity, being too focused on your appearance, neurosis, selfishness, complacency, and irresponsibility.

You are a reliable organizer

Strengths: rectitude, loyalty, sense of traditions and etiquettes, discipline, logic, sincerity, punctuality, consistency, regularity, confidence, perseverance, courage, effort, stability, and balance.

Challenges: rigidity, nervousness, fussiness, obsession, strictness, austerity, stubbornness, materialistic, closed-mindedness, perfectionism, and lack of fantasy.

You enjoy shaking things up and trying new things

Strengths: ability to change and evolve rapidly, independence, sensuality, casualness, novelty, surprise, passion, fluidity, search for balance, ease, curiosity, freedom, movement, autonomy, adaptability, charm, and seduction.

Challenges: instability, impatience, nervousness, inconsistency, carelessness, lack of balance (physically, emotionally, and psychically), bad memory, poor organizational skills, irresponsibility, and fickleness.

You are family-minded

Strengths: sense of responsibility, care, diligence, honesty, goodness, artistic taste, a taste for the finer things in life, seriousness, attention, understanding, romanticism, active listening, and good at asserting yourself by respecting your boundaries and balance.

Challenges: indecisiveness, doubt, lack of self-confidence, oversensitivity, self-doubt, struggling with taking a stance, struggles with decision making, moodiness, sacrifice, inconsistency, irregularity, and a great need for safety.

You enjoy reflection and research

Strengths: great at cultivating a rich inner life (silence, meditation), sharp intelligence, magnetism, tranquility, simplicity, rich and advanced spiritual quest, analytical skills, knowledge, quest for truth, and honesty.

Challenges: routine, secrecy, associability, melancholy, loneliness, being conservative, coldness, being closed off, discretion, shyness, frustration, denial and disconnect from reality, fantasy, daydreaming, anxiety, and fear of innovation and change.

You are great at managing

Strengths: power, fidelity, loyalty, rectitude, goodness, determination, sense of justice, success, strength, tenacity, quick and efficient worker, generosity, dynamism, enthusiasm, balance, and leadership.

Challenges: intolerance, authoritarianism, materialistic, fear of running out (of food, possessions, etc.), stubborn nature, pride, overinflated ego, harshness, being obsessed with materialistic success or fame, lack of tact, manipulation, tyranny, and struggles with expressing emotions.

You enjoy philanthropy

Strengths: ability to open up to others, great understanding, artistic talent, open-mindedness, open heart, acts of service, generosity, compassion, humanitarianism, sensitivity, sharing, empathy, and ability to advice others astutely.

Challenges: overemotional, high ideals, self-sacrifice, sacrificing others, disconnect from reality, forgetting your own needs, utopist nature, exaltation, intolerance, denial, dictatorship, idle talks, and difficulties keeping a secret.

You are an inspired medium

Strengths: ambition, inspiration, profound motivation, sharp intelligence, advanced intuition, meticulousness, inner strength, sharing ideals and divine messages, great spirituality, and large and inclusive vision.

Challenges: demanding nature, intolerance, perfectionism, closed-mindedness, selfishness, mystical delusions, being difficult to live with, strength, uncontrollable energy, God complex, and bad management of your ideas.

You enjoy leading people

Strengths: universal aspirations, humanitarianism, innovation, equity, balance, accomplishment, important realizations (especially abroad), novelty, unusual intelligence, desire to advance in life, and good leadership (with groups and communities).

Challenges: great nervousness, getting carried away, hypersensitivity, depression, dementia, intense inner turmoil, excessive nature, duality, obsession, struggles with channeling your inspiration and energy, emotional instability, daydreaming.

You are great at meditation

Strengths: rare and exceptional qualities, wisdom, humanitarianism, intelligence, selflessness, goodness, tolerance, respect, compassion, conciliation, grace, softness, ironclad reliability.

Challenges: abuse of power, irresponsibility and avoidance, misanthropy, being easily offended, inferiority complex, victimization, and fear of failure and abandonment.

THE HIDDEN SELF

The hidden self is the sum of all the consonants of the first name and family name.

For Anne-Sophie Casper:

$$5 + 5 + 1 + 7 + 8 + 3 + 1 + 7 + 9 = 46 = 4 + 6 = 10 = 1 + 0 = 1$$

Write your hidden self number here: _____

The hidden self is also called the intimate number. This numbers tells you about the unconscious aspects of your personality, it refers to the ways you can realize your materialistic and professional life. It represents the fuel, power, and energy you will need to use to reach your life goals. It is often associated with the aspiration number. The intimate number is the unconscious urge of your own self who, through its influence, pushes you to accomplish your destiny, to become who you are meant to be. The core of the hidden self is what must be done and accomplished in your life.

It's also your professional accomplishments, what you must do in your current incarnation's field. The hidden self is like the hidden core of your own family. It represents your deepest nature, nestled deep within yourself.

IF YOU GET THE NUMBER:

You are a dynamic leader

You need to lead, be active and independent, and achieve things on your own. A true leader, you are a driven and dynamic person, with great analytical, organizational, and deductive skills. You work best alone because you don't easily trust others.

You are an attentive adviser

You need to collaborate, work, and share with others. It is vital for you to interact with others because loneliness doesn't suit you. You are an emotional, sensitive, intuitive, and insightful person. Equality is important to you, and you possess a sort of naïve fragility that can lead to misunderstanding.

You are an original creator

You need to create, communicate, share, and express yourself. You must share your creative energy with the world in any way you can. You like being independent. You are versatile by nature, but be careful to not scatter yourself, and watch out for inconsistency and loss of focus. These things could steer you away from your first aspirations.

You are a reassuring anchor

You need things to be done properly, with the right method and in an orderly fashion. Structure is an essential part of your work ethics. You are a sturdy, methodical, stable, and focused person, and you primarily look for security in life. But do not forget to be more casual, innocent, and carefree in life.

You are a free spirit
You need to travel and be constantly moving. Your biggest enemy is routine. Your great versatility allows you to be clever, independent, mobile, and quick on your toes. Sharp-minded and curious, you have an innate gift for persuasion, but you struggle with rejection.

You are a born mediator
You need to be accommodating and resolve and appease conflicts, especially within your family. You are good at creating a peaceful and calm atmosphere. With your responsible and organized nature, you solve every problem (or close enough), in accordance with your own ideals. Remember to respect the natural order of things, because not everything can be controlled and perfect.

You are a solitary thinker
You need to think, analyze, study, diagnose, and advise. You are a culturally and spiritually rich person. Independent and organized, you like to spend time alone, focusing on your personal research or your precise work. But do not isolate yourself by getting stuck in a strange melancholy.

You are a practical maker
You need to develop your tangible and realistic sense of initiative. You value efficiency, determination, and power to achieve your goals. Without these traits, you are quickly overwhelmed by your own great personal power. You have a great gift for business, exchanges, and transactions, no matter their nature. However, don't forget that other people possess similar skills.

You are a devoted altruist

You need to communicate within a group or a community, for this is where you belong. You express yourself through great acts of service, listening, and self-sacrifice. Your ability to relieve, help, and support others is admirable. But be careful, for these abilities can help discover the world as much as they can dissociate you from reality.

You are an inspiring visionary

You need to create to pass down the inspiring messages you harbor, but you also need to lead others. Driven by your magnetic and powerful energy, you embark on the most perilous journeys with confidence, bravery, and determination. You always come through, even though your rhythm is irregular, demanding, and hard to follow.

You are a global entrepreneur

You need to express you passion for great projects in order to calmly reach your high ideals. Self-revelation and the realization of others can be achieved through great constructions. But to realize your great power of construction, you must be meticulous and perfectly master your personal ambition.

You are a humanitarian guide

You need to commit to others to lead groups and entire communities with a masterful hand. You possess a bright and magnetic aura, dedicated to your wisdom, compassion, and kindness. Your high-level and demanding responsibilities require you to always be exemplary, no matter what.

ENLIGHTENED CALCULATIONS

✦

In addition to the basic identity calculations we covered, which only apply to your surnames and family names, I now suggest you deepen your knowledge with the enlightened calculations. To calculate these, you will need some of your previous results, as well as your date of birth. Remember that no number is only good or bad. Each result is made of two parts: the strengths (the positive aspect) and the challenges (the negative aspect). To have a global vision of all your results, don't forget to fill in the numbers on the following pages.

THE SPIRITUAL INITIATION

The spiritual initiation is calculated by adding the aspiration number + expression number + life path + date of birth.

0	5	0	1	1	9	8	5	$29 = 11$

The life path, which I explain in the life calculations (p. 84), is calculated by adding all the numbers in your day of birth.

For instance, for Anne-Sophie Casper, born January 5, 1985:

$$1 + 5 + 1 + 9 + 8 + 5 = 29 = 2 + 9 = 11$$

For Anne-Sophie Casper, the spiritual initiation is then:

$$5 + 6 + 11 + 5 = 27 = 2 + 7 = 9$$

Write your spiritual initiation number here: _____

The spiritual initiation is the life lesson that will enlighten the aspiration number we previously calculated. This number represents a great inner challenge, linked to our many realizations through life. The spiritual initiation is synonymous with personal growth, the school of life. It also represents the times life needs to kick you so you can evolve.

IF YOU GET THE NUMBER:

Your biggest challenge is opening up

Strengths: leadership, strength, self-determination, charisma, independence, self-assertion, exploration, creativity, activity, bursts of energy, boldness, dynamism, self-confidence, and a sharp and quick mind.

Challenges: loneliness, stubbornness, individualism, pretentiousness, exuberance, lies, cunning, charlatanism, authority, intolerance, greed, selfishness, rigidity, and excess of confidence.

Your biggest obstacle in life is duality

Strengths: association, compatibility, balance, cooperation, conciliation, motion, tranquil growth, temperance, intuitive sensitivity, imagination, listening, diplomacy, tenderness, sociability, team spirit, and warmth.

Challenges: regression, passivity, naïveté, lack of confidence, self-doubt, oversensitivity, being overemotional, instability, negligence, inferiority complex, dependency, shyness, daydreaming, and nonchalance.

Your biggest challenge is focusing

Strengths: self-expression, spontaneity, sociability, extroversion, seduction, intelligence, elegance, persuasion, confidence, expansiveness, creativity, dynamism, joie de vivre, freshness, sensitivity, and communication.

Challenges: immaturity, naïveté, infantilism, disobedience, jealousy, instability, pretentiousness, aggressivity, pride, vanity, passing fancies, depression, self-doubt, and manipulation.

Your biggest obstacle in life is inflexibility

Strengths: work, reliability, groundedness, endurance, patience, organization, stability, structure, bravery, resilience, determination, good everyday management, security, methodism, discipline, and respecting the rules.

Challenges: rigidity, being too controlling, intolerance, ambitiousness, fear, slowness, limitation, mental blocks, extreme perfectionism, pessimism, struggle, overprotection, mental, psychic and physical imprisonment, inflexibility, routine, and lack of freedom and creativity.

Your biggest challenge is instability

Strengths: curiosity, discovery, motion, freedom, independence, adaptability, adventurous mind, energy, boldness, sensuality, communication, vivacity, sharing, flexibility, independence, happiness, charm, open-mindedness, experimentation, optimism, enthusiasm, research, and inventiveness.

Challenges: intolerance, inconsistency, being easily offended, zealotry, impatience, impulsivity, carelessness, inhibition, incoherence, important changes (changing your mind, jobs, partners, countries, etc.), competitiveness, infidelity, provocation, exaggeration, nervousness, scattered mind, waste of time and energy, unpredictability, fatigue, and anxiety.

Your biggest obstacle in life is extreme perfectionism

Strengths: patience, seeing the whole picture, forgiveness, acceptance (of yourself and others), objective judgment, responsibility, family, healing, balance, love, sense of justice, sensuality, generosity, harmony, beauty, aesthetic, refinement, idealism, and compassion.

Challenges: obsession, anxiety, fear, loose morals, holding grudges, naïveté, discretion, being overly critical, demanding nature, irresponsibility, impatience, idealization, self-sacrifice, jealousy, anger, fear of conflicts, and hesitation.

Your biggest challenge is overthinking

Strengths: spirituality, brainpower, expertise, originality, curiosity, wisdom, intuition, being perceptive and analytical, self-control, self-analysis, hardworking, focus, inwardness, reflection, understanding, serenity, innate ability to learn, think and study.

Challenges: loneliness, self-exclusion, being too controlling, aloofness, tyranny, emotional blocks, authoritarianism, zealotry, intellectual and nervous burnout, domineering nature, closed-mindedness, misanthropy, pride, marginality, superiority complex, and excess or lack of self-confidence.

Your biggest obstacle in life is excess of power

Strengths: construction, ambition, creation, balance, bravery, combativeness, efficiency, realism, organization, productivity, practicality, transformation, rebirth, determination, justice, strategy, strength (especially physical), good business sense, hardworking, and ability to help others rebuild themselves.

Challenges: stubbornness, selfishness, manipulation, insensitivity, competitiveness, opportunism, violence, ambitiousness, lack of balance, frustration, egocentricity, domineering personality, extreme self-assertion, dishonesty, provocation, brutality, corruption, arrogance, decadence, destruction, jealousy, sadism, and God complex.

Your biggest challenge is utopia

Strengths: brotherhood, humaneness, an open consciousness, commitment, understanding, compassion, intuition, truthfulness, universality, tolerance, devotion, transmission, deepness, charisma, wisdom, loyalty, clairvoyance, and altruism.

Challenges: sacrifice, being overemotional, great nervousness, idealism, zealotry, dependency, being unrealistic, anxiety, disconnect from reality, sensitivity, loneliness, naïveté, lying, inner fragility, and bad at listening (to yourself and others).

Your biggest obstacle in life is manipulation

Strengths: mediumship, channeling, high stock of energy, good at surpassing yourself, advanced intuition, creativity, excellent communication, confidence, magnetism, inspiration, teaching, fertility, independence, idealism, dynamism, spirituality, premonition, charisma, ability to convey things, pedagogy, intelligence of the heart and mind.

Challenges: deep inner duality, rebellion, authoritarianism, tyranny, cunning, egocentricity, lack of confidence, stubbornness, selfishness, anxiety, self-destruction, self-importance, loneliness, doubts, fears, great mental blocks, apathy, depression, jealousy, bipolar nature, misuse of intelligence, and dependency.

Your biggest challenge is using your incredible energy right

Strengths: global ambition, determination, intuition, creation, energy, magnetism, discipline, cooperation, construction, pragmatism, confidence, willpower, hardworking, great ideals, ability to accomplish great things, balance, and ability to surpass yourself and build things for others.

Challenges: defeatism, megalomania, inner duality, authoritarianism, insecurity, self-destruction, depression, tyranny, paralysis, egocentricity, selfishness, utopist, jealousy, lack of confidence, fears, and phobias.

Your biggest obstacle in life is self-sacrifice

Strengths: creative expression, optimism, excellent communication, belief, persuasion, high ideals, leadership, education intelligence, confidence, open-mindedness, humanitarianism, inspiration, mediumship, acceptance (of yourself and others), seeing the whole picture, ability to express your emotions, and ability to understand a project beforehand.

Challenges: self-destruction, fear of conflict, anger, shyness, stubbornness, perfectionism, resentment, giving up, being overly critical (of yourself and others), depression, manipulation, and ability to influence the masses to satisfy your own agenda.

THE FORCE NUMBER

The force number is the addition of the birth day with the birth month.
For Anne-Sophie Casper, born January 5:

$$5 + 1 = 6.$$

Write your force number here: _____

It's your inner power, your joker card. It can also be called the soul's key. It represents the mission you have on earth in this current life. It's your spine, your motor, your motivations, your true needs, and what gives your actions meaning.

WHAT IS THE DIFFERENCE BETWEEN THE ASPIRATION NUMBER AND THE FORCE NUMBER? The aspiration number reveals how you need to accomplish yourself in life. It represents the trajectory you must take, especially once you turn thirty-five. The force number, however, relates to the main mission you will have throughout your life.

IF YOU GET THE NUMBER:

You are a visionary leader

Your success must be lived alone. Your mission is to transform people, ideas, concepts, and companies so they can grow and fully realize themselves. It is important that you take charge of your life to make the right decisions.

You are a gifted caretaker

Collaboration and dual work are essential to you. Your mission is to help, protect, and assist people, projects, and structures so they can evolve and shine. It is important that you cultivate confidence and determination to succeed with your teammates.

You are a communicating creative

Self-expression and being open to the world are essential things to you. Your mission is to weave and repair relations between people, in your family, at school, at the office, or within a community. It is important that you cultivate your creativity every day, no matter what you do.

You are a resistant builder

Because you are persistent and organized, structured and methodical work is essential. You have a particularly efficient gentle strength. Your mission is to build long-term, strong, and safe things. It is important that you take your time to think and realize your goals.

You are a free thinker

You have the potential of a trailblazer for whom innovation, mobility, and independence are essential. Propelled by the energy of movement and novelty, your mission is to bring your personal energy to the world in order to transform it positively and help humanity mourn its losses (natural disasters, health crises, etc.).

You are a kind therapist

You have the potential of a great caretaker for whom wellness, harmony, and balance are essential. Your mission is heavy and demanding. Most of you act as parents for your own parents, for you weren't supported by them in your youth. It is essential for you to create a sense of family in every group you join.

You are an attentive adviser

You have the potential of an original consultant for whom reflection, analysis, curiosity, and observation are essential. You must use your difference and your singularity as tools to help you research, understand, and advise. Your delicate mission is to transmit your teachings to as many people as possible.

You are a long-term builder

You have the potential of a powerful builder to whom balance, energy, and strength are essential. Your mission is to use your power in order to help achieve ambitious projects. It is essential that you take your place in the world without waiting for others to do it for you.

You are a curious altruist

You have the potential of a humanitarian to whom the understanding of the world, in the broad sense of the term, is essential. Your mission is to develop and fully express your talents in order to pass them down to humankind. It is important that your dreams always lead you to birth an idea or a project, or to defend a cause or a community.

You are an inspired guide

Intuition and *energy* are your watchwords. You are endowed with an inner strength that drives you to action, and you easily take others with you. Your mission is to go above and beyond to guide others and help them succeed in their projects, implement their ideas, and realize their life ideals. Be careful not to put your incredible resources solely at the service of your own interests.

You are a connected visionary

Your feelings, intuition, and, in particular, energy are your gifts. Your mission is to develop your perception skills and surpass yourself in order to build incredible things (physical, artistic, etc.). Never stay inactive. Feed your powerful inner resources, your gift, and your innate qualities in order to serve the collective.

You are a magnetic leader

Understanding, respecting others, wisdom, and compassion are essential to you. You attract the masses, and you commit yourself body and soul to your mission. That is a rare quality, and can be incredibly draining. It is important that you use all your wisdom, gifts, and kindness to help all of humankind.

LIFE CALCULATIONS

✦

Now that you have your identity and enlightened numbers, I invite you to explore your life path. Its calculation, only based on your date of birth, is relatively simple. And yet, it is very important.

Let me remind you that no number is simply good or bad. Each result is made of four parts: the keywords, the goal, the gifts (positive aspect), and the limitations (negative aspect). To see the general overview of your results, don't forget to fill out the numbers on the following pages.

THE LIFE PATH

The life path details your initial journey and its purpose, environment, climate, and events. This calculation will help you decipher your personality and understand how to accomplish your goals in all the areas of your life, all while developing your resources and qualities without ignoring your weaknesses and limitations. Thanks to the life path, you will more easily ascertain your missions, goals, and the most fulfilling direction to take in life. This is all determined at your birth, and your profound personality will follow you until your death. It can be reinforced and fed during fulfilling times in your life, or it can be diminished, even asleep (during a depression for example). But whatever happens, it will always be there, waiting to be revealed!

To calculate the life path, add the day, month, and year of birth.

For instance, for Anne-Sophie Casper, born January 5, 1985:

$$1 + 5 + 1 + 9 + 8 + 5 = 29 = 2 + 9 = 11$$

Write your life path number here: _____

IF YOU GET THE NUMBER:

1

You are an enterprising and creative motivator

Keywords: dynamism, lonely achievements, personal successes, individuality, action, ambition, creativity, confidence, boldness, great energy, strength, bravery, willpower, self-confidence or lack of self-confidence, competitiveness, and destructive and addictive behavior (affective addiction, drug, alcohol, food).

Goal: Stepping away from your insecurities and well-hidden inferiority complex.

Gifts:
- Surpassing yourself and inspiring others to do the same.
- Guiding, leading, and showing leadership skill.
- Expressing your talents (art and creation).
- Being independent; freedom of thought and action is essential.

Limitations:
- Individualism and egocentricity.
- Nervousness, irritability, and impatience.
- Authoritarianism and intolerance.

You are a loyal and committed support

Keywords: calm, harmony, mediator, balance, associations, collaboration, patience, diplomacy, cooperation, fulfilling alliance, favorable union, inferiority complex, affective dependency, being too critical (of yourself and others), duality, and strong inner conflicts.

Goal: Supporting and helping others without acting like a savior.

Gifts:
- Helping others in an honest, genuine, and sincere way.
- Being the attentive ear to whom one confides easily.
- Acting as a mediator within a group.
- Sharing your sense of compromise and consensus.

Limitations:
- Oversensitivity and shyness.
- Paralyzing fear of conflict and criticism.
- Avoiding confrontation in fear of being hurt.

You are sensitive and constructive speaker

Keywords: creative resources, rapidness, expression, emotion, joy, openness, extroversion, optimism, authenticity, artistic talent, self-sacrifice, sharing your sensitivity, determination, fatigue, creating interactions with others.

Goal: Unlocking your positive thinking to stimulate your emotional expression.

Gifts:
- Suggesting innovative ideas; cultivating a strong network.
- Communicating in a genuine and inspired way.
- Putting your optimism in service of the world.
- Being loyal and helpful.

Limitations:
- Alternating phases of ups and downs, which can overtime lead to depression.
- Irresponsibility, nonchalance, and immaturity.
- Quirkiness and shallowness; the need to be in the spotlight shouldn't be a priority.

You are a reliable and organized builder

Keywords: structure, solidity, work, construction, professional success, discipline, rigor, regularity, consistent efforts, bravery, seriousness, tenacity, perseverance, material security, unusual determination, rigidity, being too focused, and lack of flexibility.

Goal: Overcoming your deepest fears in order to gradually reach a state of harmony between rationality and emotions.

Gifts:
- Building solid foundations (material, relational, etc.).
- Stabilizing and solidifying (things, people, relationships, ideas, etc.).
- Analyzing and following directions, a technique, a rule, a method or a specific setting.
- Working relentlessly.

Limitations:
- Routine and an overly rational mind; accepting the unexpected can also mean opening up to life's beautiful surprises.
- Rigidity, closed-mindedness, and aloofness, due to a lack of fantasy.
- A sedentary lifestyle and boredom, for you are stuck in your fears and doubts.

5 You are a free and independent adventurer

Keywords: exploration, motion, adventure, freedom, independence, variety, mobility, travels (physical, spiritual, philosophical . . .), changes, novelty, diversity, metamorphosis, good health (mental, physical and psychic), mandatory discipline, necessary self-control in order to reach inner peace.

Goal: Living your current incarnation's life intensely and deeply.

Gifts:
- Being flexible and adaptable.
- Being bold and curious.
- Expressing your freedom and inspiring others to do the same.
- Broadening your horizons and your set of references in order to find unexpected solutions.

Limitations:
- Scattering yourself and trying to do too many things at once.
- Impulsivity and dependency (affective dependency, drugs or alcohol addiction, etc.).
- Egocentricity and frustration.

6 You are an aesthetic idealist

Keywords: love, home, family, compassion, acceptance, openness, harmony, alliance, union, conciliation, adaptability, responsibility, national destiny, apparent success, chaotic journey, doubt (of yourself and others), hesitation, willpower, generosity, sharing, and compassion.

Goal: Searching for spiritual enlightenment in order to sow seeds of happiness.

Gifts:
- Creating harmonious, nice, and warm ambiances.
- Guiding, leading, and actively listening in order to better things.
- Taking care of others by granting them all of your attention.
- Communicating with authenticity and kindness.

Limitations:
- Helping others at the risk of forgetting about yourself.
- Inserting yourself in other people's lives, sometimes feeding off their difficulties and misfortunes.
- Perfectionism, jealousy, and envy.

You are a perceptive and generous thinker

Keywords: independence, research, originality, analytical skills, reflection, studies of the mind, knowledge, spirituality, esoterism, psychology, wisdom, transmission, lack of curiosity, being perceptive, discretion, love, faith, loving nature, loneliness, difficult union, and isolation.

Goal: Accomplishing yourself as a researcher, teacher, psychologist, or doctor.

Gifts:
- Thinking, analyzing, and questioning yourself about the meaning of life.
- Developing an expertise.
- Being discreet and calm.
- Cultivating your inner world.

Limitations:
- Loneliness induced misanthropy.
- Closed-mindedness and passiveness.
- Aloofness, pretentiousness, and pride while harboring a superiority complex.

You are a successful builder

Keywords: boldness, material success, ambitious accomplishments, philanthropy, power, energy, bravery, money, endurance, perseverance, focus, fame, determination, abundance, authority, fighting introversion, abuse of power, and struggles.

Goal: Transcend abundance to serve others by shining or by remaining very discreet.

Gifts:
- Building long-term things.
- Showing great determination.
- Thinking and working hard.
- Attracting money energy to you.

Limitations:
- Being manipulative, controlling, and domineering.
- Being authoritarian and violent, verbally or physically.
- Social climber and asocial nature.

You are a charismatic seeker

Keywords: escapism, openness, multiple and varied experiences, travels, meetings, passion, commitment, integrity, wisdom, devotion, artistic sensibility, creativity, imagination, utopia, sacrifice, abnegation, and understanding yourself and others.

Goal: The search for an ideal, for a fair life that allows you to blossom into a leader.

Gifts:
- Discovering the world while nourishing your innate curiosity.
- Radiating your magnetic energy.
- Being an inspiring example for others.

Limitations:
- Hypersensitivity and being overemotional.
- Zealotry and selfishness.
- Obsessive mindset and negativity.

You are a very creative channel

Keywords: originality, surpassing yourself, ambitious accomplishments, atypical projects, surprising everyday life, dynamism, inspiration, control, magnetic energy, innate charisma, ironclad determination, intelligence, creativity, confidence, intuition, frustration, limitation, restriction, and intense nature.

Goal: Using your intuition, creative energy, and confidence to help others.

Gifts:
- Listening to your inner voice and cultivating your spirituality.
- Guiding and helping others to grow and radiate.
- Inventing and creating ideas and concepts to make them evolve.
- Reaching your ambitious goals thanks to your great willpower.

Limitations:
- Demanding and perfectionist nature, toward yourself and others.
- Authoritarianism, controlling and tyrannical nature.
- Individualism with a God complex.

You are a brilliant and ambitious visionary

Keywords: large-scale achievements, important projects, ambitious constructions, energy, practical intelligence, magnetism, powerful vibrations, openness, developing your healing gifts, intense activity, hobbies, and rare pleasures.

Goal: Merge your energy with your intuition to play a big role in the creation of a better world.

Gifts:
- Understanding the world and adapting to difference in the broad sense.
- Building and erecting important things.
- Inventing, creating, and innovating.
- Surpassing yourself by using your incredible inner resources.

Limitations:
- Being afraid of leaving your comfort zone.
- Selfishness, materialistic mindset and individualism.
- Being closed-off and depressed.

You are an inspired and innovative sage

Keywords: elevated vision, high ambition, empathy, great aspirations, wisdom, maturity, sensitivity, compassion, innate luck, success, fear, doubt, hesitation, frustration, stress, being too critical, obsessive, and perfectionism.

Goal: Exceed your life experience to inspire others to do the same.

Gifts:
- Expressing your innovative and original ideas.
- Sharing and communicating in a genuine and inspired way.
- Cultivating your healing gifts.
- Being loyal, faithful, and helpful.

Limitations:
- Alternating phases of ups and downs that can quickly lead to depression.
- Sensitivity, devotion, and addictions (alcohol, drugs, etc.).
- Perfectionism, superiority complex, and egocentricity.

THE PERSONAL YEAR

The personal year number is helpful in evaluating the trend of the coming year. You can then actively cultivate all your assets by maximizing the positive aspects of the year, but also be aware of the coming obstacles and challenges and thus properly deal with the limitations you might be confronted with. If your personal year number is the same as your life path number, it means that your life path's interpretation and its influences are heightened.

People sometimes say that the personal year is calculated from your birthday, and that is when it takes effect, similar to how they calculate the sun revolution in astrology, but that's false.

In numerology, each personal year starts on January 1 and ends on December 31, no matter your date of birth. Starting from November 11, we all enter a time of transition during which we become more familiar with the vibration of our new numerological cycle (which starts on the following January 1).

To calculate the personal year, add the day and month of your birth with the year you wish to analyze.

In 2022 (which was effective in November 2021), the personal year of Anne-Sophie Casper, born January 5, will be:

$$1 + 5 + 2 + 0 + 2 + 2 = 12 = 1 + 2 = 3$$

Write your personal life number here: _____

IF YOU GET THE NUMBER:

This is the most important year

This year marks the beginning of a nine-year cycle; it represents the foundations upon which you will build everything for the next eight years. Assert your personality, begin new ambitious projects, set important things in motion, and be determined.

Step out of your comfort zone with confidence by training for a new job, asking for a transfer, starting your own company, or moving out. Everything you will build during this first year will last throughout the cycle.

My advice: Even if you feel alone, stay positive, committed, and bold by trying hard to convert your aspirations into tangible actions.

This is the year for collaboration and teamwork

During year 2, creativity, harmony, cooperation, and sharing are important. The ongoing projects you started the previous year will carry on with similar vibrations. During year 2, we welcome associations, unions, and weddings, but also breakups and divorces. Feelings and emotions can become smothering. If this is the case, make some compromise and accept that you have to live through this duality and frustration. If this doesn't apply to you, fully enjoy the harmony, balance, and stability in your life.

My advice: Accept outside help, and be patient and tolerant. This will help you create more fulfilling communication skills.

This is the perfect year for socialization

Year 3 is the year for connections, exchanges, and friendships. Take advantage of this year to reconnect. This is also a transitional year during which you might have to mourn. Year 3 can close the first third of the nine-year cycle on a light note, with activities, pleasures, and recreation taking center stage. Even if you are feeling stress, year 3 could represent a beneficial reassessment.

My advice: Feed your creativity, for it is particularly fertile (the birth of a child, an art piece, a project, etc.).

This is the year for construction or destruction

After the pleasures and frivolities of year 3, year 4 is more arduous. It is not rare to come across obstacles, limitations, accidents, or depression. To face this year of hard work (or forced rest), rely on order, structure, and organization. Deal with your affairs by staying determined, flexible, and motivated. Year 4 tries your sense of initiative, your responsiveness, your practicality, and your ability to focus in order to gain a better emotional intelligence.

My advice: Because the vibrations of the 4th personal year are not great, keep an eye on your work, finances, and health.

This is the year for freedom and adventure

Year 5 is very favorable for encounters, new experiences, changes, house moves, and travel. But watch out for the unnecessary risks that could lead to accidents at home or while you're traveling. Your personal vibrations are excellent and favorable for abundance and creation (childbirth, new job, higher revenues, etc.).

My advice: In order to evolve positively, leave your comfort zone to seize the opportunities, possibilities, and surprises of life.

This year is perfect for family and money

Adapting to family obligations (birth, marriage, divorce, separation) is essential during year 6. Generally speaking, if you're in a happy relationship, this year should be a year of shared happiness. However, if this is a prickly subject, year 6 will require you to take a stand and make choices about your home. If you fully take responsibility, you will get beautiful professional successes. The 6th year of the numerological cycle offers you three paths: the two paths of the extremes and the middle path, the path of balance. You decide which path is right for you.

My advice: If people owe you money, ask to get it back in order to invest (new car, buying a house, etc.).

7

This is a year for self-reflection

Away from others, you are thinking, planning, contemplating, and summarizing. This year could look like a time for rest, but the truth is very different. Inner activity will be very intense. Explore psychology, esoterism, and spirituality by cultivating patience and determination.

Unions, projects, and financial investments are not favorable. However, negative events might surprise you (losing a job that wasn't fulfilling, losing touch with someone who depended too much on your money or energy, etc.). They might quickly turn out to be beneficial for your growth.

My advice: Bet on your personal reflection by taking a step back to obverse your life plans.

This is the year to reap what you have sowed

Year 8 is very favorable for finances, legal matters, signing contracts or leases, and justice in the general sense. You will reap positive things and money. Your efforts will be rewarded. You can yet assert yourself in your job and accomplish projects that seemed impossible until then.

During year 8, successes and failures are enhanced. Always remain humble and realistic, for stress management and impatience can be intense. In the numerological cycle, this is the year that will attract ambition, materialism, and workaholism. It favors actions meant to better communities, groups, or humankind. It is essential that you use your power and strength to accomplish yourself fully and help others do the same.

My advice: Pay attention to your health, for frequent trips to the hospital might be needed.

9

This year announces endings

Year 9 is the time to assess and appraise. You must analyze every aspect (financial, educative, medical, etc.) of your life and finalize your projects. During this year, it's recommended to end contracts, companies, relationships, and associations that are no longer fulfilling and nourishing. Let go of the things that don't belong anymore. This will give you enough room to welcome new things.

It is also a good time to fix things and take care of yourself. During this time, you will reap what you sowed during the past eight years. Long-distance business relationships and friendships will be favored. A new lifestyle will slowly develop in order to offer you new possibilities and start a new cycle. Anticipate the future in an ambitious and bold way in order to prepare strong foundations for the next coming years.

My advice: Since nothing will last, don't start new activities, personal or professional.

11

This is the year for emotions

This year is particularly intense since it is carried by the vibration of a master number. The probability that you will have to live an 11 year is slim, because usually its vibrations turn into the vibrations of year 2, which is a lot calmer. I must concede that a year carried by a master number's vibration is more powerful than one carried by a classic number (1 to 9). A year with the number 11 will be very emotional. Managing energy, tension, and excess (big ups and big downs) is the main challenge of this year. Inspiration, revelation, intuition, creativity, sensibility, inner strength, and combativeness are the keywords of the year 11.

You must cultivate great self-control by putting new ideals into practice. Do not remain self-centered, or the great energetic potential of this master number may be wasted.

My advice: Success is mostly about personal growth, spirituality, literature, or art.

This is the year of absolute openness

Year 22 is just as intense as year 11 since it's also carried by the vibrations of a master number. The probability that you will have to live a 22 year is very unlikely, for the vibrations of the number 22 usually transform into the number 4. I must concede that a year carried by a master number's vibration is more powerful than one carried by a classic number (1 to 9). A year with the number 22 will be very challenging. The constructive or destructive aspects of year 4 of the cycle are enhanced. If lived deeply, year 22 possesses all of the vibrations of year 11, but doubled.

All the things you undertake during year 22 must be beneficial to society, a community, or humankind. Selflessness must be absolute. Shallowness, vanity, and fame don't belong here. Organize your skills, talents, and qualities in order to help your friends, colleagues, and even larger circles. If you are self-centered, the energetic potential of this master number will be nonexistent.

My advice: Be incredibly patient toward others, yourself, and life.

This an exceptional year

Another very intense year, much like the years 11 and 22, since it is yet again carried by the vibrations of a master number. The probability that you will have to live a 33 year is very unlikely, for the vibrations of the number 33 usually transform into the number 6. I must concede that a year carried by a master number's vibration is more powerful than one carried by a classic number (1 to 9). A year with the number 33 will be very intense.

If you do live it, year 33 will possess all the vibrations of the years 11 and 22, but enhanced. I invite you to read them again calmly, in order to assimilate each element. Quite the program awaits you! This year could be decisive for your personal and professional growth. The realizations and advancements you will undertake will be giant steps in your life path. If you are selfish or manipulate others for your personal gain, it could completely waste the energetic potential of this master number.

My advice: Always turn outward (toward others, society, and the world).

VIBRATORY CALCULATIONS

✦

In addition to the identity, enlightened and life calculations, I am inviting you to now discover the vibratory calculations of months and days. Their calculation is extremely simple and quick. But don't forget that numbers aren't just good or bad. Each result is thus made of two parts: the keywords (positive and negative), and my advice. To have a broad vision of all your results, don't forget to fill out the numbers on the following pages.

THE MONTH VIBRATIONS

The month number is useful for knowing the trend of the 28th, 29th, 30th, 31st, or upcoming days. During these days, you can actively cultivate all your assets by maximizing all the month's positive aspects and knowing its obstacles and challenges. You may then accordingly deal with the limitations you may face. If the month number is identical to your birth month, then its interpretation and influences will be enhanced. There are two ways to calculate the month vibrations.

The first one (which I use the most for month vibrations and the month of birth of my consultants) consists of associating the month's spot in the calendar to its number.

For example: 1 = January, 2 = February, up until number = 11 (this is a master number we don't reduce) and December = 12 = 1 + 2 = 3 (a special 3; see the description for 12 below).

For the second method, you will need the Pythagorean alphabet below (see p. 29) in order to transform the month's letters into numbers (from 1 to 9 or 11).

1	2	3	4	5	6	7	8	9
A	B	C	D	E	F	G	H	I
J	K	L	M	N	O	P	Q	R
S	T	U	V	W	X	Y	Z	

For example, January = $1 + 1 + 5 + 4 + 9 + 5 + 9 = 34 = 3 + 4 = 7$

Write your current month number here: _____

Write your birth month number here: _____

IF YOU GET THE NUMBER:

The month of boldness

Keywords: independence, determination, legacy, ability to easily teach, dexterity, and masculine energy.

My advice: Stay in the now, without thinking about the past or anticipating the future.

The month of openness

Keywords: open-mindedness and an open heart, strong influence of the mother, creativity, freedom, and dependency.

My advice: Free yourself and let go of the pressure your mother (or another woman in your life) exerts on you.

The month of artistic expression

Keywords: inspiration, creativity, imagination, calmness, tolerance, peace, sociability, and expression.

My advice: Take some time to practice and develop your artistic gifts (theater, singing, dancing, music, painting, drawing, etc.)

The month of hard work

Keywords: hard work, limitation, need for recognition and attention, restriction, and frustration.

My advice: Increase your personal energy levels by taking plenty of recuperative breaks.

The month of renewal

Keywords: motion, pleasure, entertainment, change, active social life, sexuality, and irregularity.

My advice: Take advantage of spring to do a big clean up in your life. Only keep the things, places, activities, and relationships that bring you joy.

The month of indecisiveness

Keywords: shyness, sensitivity, ambivalence, softness, kindness, reserve, obligations, and discretion.

My advice: Little by little, step out of your shell and discover the world outside of your comfort zone.

The month of adventure

Keywords: spontaneity, natural, travels, studies, extroversion, relations, communication, and reflection.

My advice: Learn how to balance your need for social life and your need for introspection.

The month of balance

Keywords: work, power, leadership, stability, fragility, impulsivity, quick stances, jealousy, and logic.

My advice: Remain calm when faced with events and situations that can shake up your everyday life.

The month of emotiveness

Keywords: success, oversensitivity, hurt (from an injustice, a betrayal, a humiliation or a rejection), perfectionism, amiability, sensuality, and creativity.

My advice: You can sometimes struggle to adapt, but your efforts are not in vain. Keep going and stick to your values and principles.

The month of change

Keywords: motion, independence, activity, instability, friendship, chatting, positivity, and charm.

My advice: To avoid going under, surf on the wave of change as best as you can.

The month of combativity

Keywords: discretion, reserve, nervousness, vitality, struggle, activity, strong personality, and etiquette.

My advice: Everything you struggle against will persist. Preserve your beautiful energy by letting go of the things that are not worth it.

The month of generosity

Keywords: self-sacrifice, openness, bravery, freedom, originality, lucidity, aloofness, expression, and creativity.

My advice: Enjoy the end of the year, amass memories, and share good moments (dates, family dinners, weekend with friends, etc.).

THE DAILY VIBRATIONS

The daily number is useful in order to know the trend of the upcoming twenty-four hours. During these hours, you may then cultivate your best qualities and overcome more easily the obstacles and challenges of life. If the daily number is identical to your day of birth, its interpretation and influences will be enhanced.

Always reduce the result of your calculations to a number from 1 to 9 or one of the master numbers, 11, 22, or 33. For instance, the 31st is 3 + 1 = 4, and the 10th is 1 + 0 = 1

Write your current day number here: _____
Write your birth day number here: _____

IF YOU GET THE NUMBER:

The day of the leader

Boldness, leadership, and success are even stronger if this is the 1st day of the month (but not the 10th). Your day will be active, dynamic, and productive. This day is very beneficial for passionate, bold, and determined persons. But remember to stay humble, understanding, and open to others.

The day of associations

Your good manners are in the spotlight today. You are empathetic and logical, and you easily understand the people around you. This pacifying energy favors alliances, contracts, unions, and teamwork.

The day of communication

Contacts, exchanges, creativity, and sharing are the core of this pleasant and fulfilling day (especially emotionally). Cultivate your curiosity, your soft sensitivity, and your open-mindedness; they will bring you a lot of joy today.

The day of lasting creations

Don't be afraid to be too demanding, especially toward yourself. You can rest assured that your efforts and hard work will pay off. Stay determined, assertive, and focused. Evaluate all the opportunities, for they will bring you material stability, innovative adventures, or long-term foundations.

The day of motions
Freedom, fulfillment, the art of words, and freedom are enhanced on the 5th day of the month (but not the 14th or 23rd). Your day will be full of changes, travel, and exploration (inward and outward). Luck will also be on your side, so try a lottery ticket.

The day of confidence
Security, reliability, balance, and responsibility are the core of this day. Success, career growth, and financial success tend to happen on the 6th, 15th, and 24th of the month. Don't neglect your family, and remember to be flexible, compassionate, and empathetic with them.

The day of introspection
Your spirituality and independence are in the spotlight today. Sentimental relationships can be fragile, and evolutions can be slow, especially professionally. Take advantage of this day to study and focus on your research. They could lead you to a great success.

The day of power
Today, your growth is taking a leap forward. Financial growth, leadership growth, material growth, and friendships are important on the 8th, 17th, and 26th of the month. Know how to work hard and negotiate accordingly.

The day of important accomplishments

Great accomplishments, fame, and success (especially publicly) are even stronger if this is the 9th of the month (but not the 18th or 27th). This day favors sensitive, generous, and empathetic people. But remember to stay grounded, for unions and relationships could be fleeting.

The day of intuition

Your ability to channel things (information, energy), your skills and ambitions are in the spotlight today. You are smart, charismatic, and creative, but imperfect. Cool down your loud, frank, and determined personality. You could be overwhelmed by your own intuitive energy.

The day of great accomplishments

Your creative energy and intelligence are on top today. Family relations, mediations, and generous acts are also important. Broaden your vision and learn how to build projects on solid foundations.

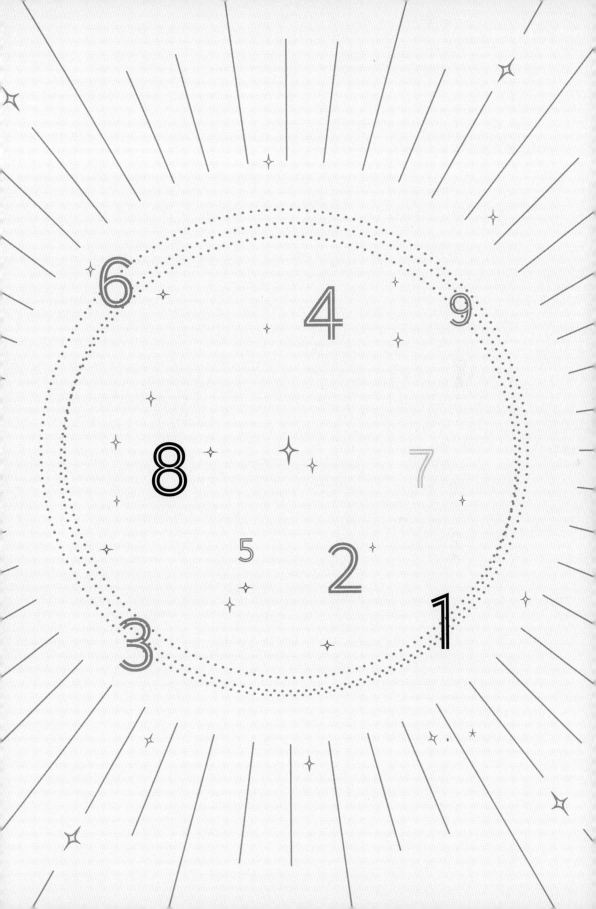

NUMEROLOGY AND THE RIGHT BRAIN

✦

THE RIGHT HEMISPHERE of your brain is in the spotlight in this fourth chapter. Intuition, sensitivity, emotion, creativity, artistic talent—so many abilities are deeply connected to your right brain. To feed it and discover this intuitive aspect of numerology, I invite you to explore elements, colors, animals, different personalities, and mirror hours. But first, take a deep dive in the fascinating world of symbolism.

INTUITIVE NUMEROLOGY

I associate intuitive numerology with the right hemisphere of the brain. The way it processes data is global, holistic, and nonsequential. This is why I am offering you an intuitive approach of numerology through symbolism, associations, and tests to complete.

NUMBERS' SYMBOLISM

✦

In this part, I will reveal my different and nonexhaustive symbolic interpretations of the numbers. They can be very subjective. They resonate within me and echo with many of the people who have consulted me. But if you don't agree with them, don't worry! It's absolutely inconsequential since—remember—intuitive numerology pushes us to discover and understand things in an unusual way. It can be unsettling if you are not used to it.

SIMPLE NUMBERS

The simple numbers are 1, 2, 3, 4, 5, 6, 7, 8, and 9. In numerology they are also called basic numbers. Besides the master numbers (11, 22, and 33), which we will explore later, they are the only numbers that must never be reduced.

1 The dynamic father

The number 1 can be written the same way in all the languages, in the shape of a staff, one straight vertical line. Its masculine energy (yang) is hard to miss. The energetic power of 1 is particularly strong and dense. This number acts by turns as a father, man, husband or partner, entrepreneur, leader, builder, trailblazer, visionary, or individualist. It reveals your masculine side and your charisma. Radiant like the sun, it represents the proud and authoritarian man. Its creative power is the base of all things. The number 1 perfectly vibrates with concepts of beginning, origin, and essence. Kind but determined, it tells you that you're ready for a fresh start. You are on the right path, so go for it without fears.

2 The kind mother

The number 2 is the first number made of a line and a curve. Graphically speaking, it perfectly symbolizes its own duality. Its feminine energy (yin) is kind. The energetic power of the 2 is particularly soft and wise. According to life's stages, it represents the mother, the wife or partner, but also the feminine part of ourselves (of our divine feminine or the sensitive men), the reliable, and the adviser. The soft and harmonious vibrations for the 2 are similar to the moon, and together they create a united duo. The number 2 symbolizes the evolution of your conscience, the greatness of your soul. Despite sorrow and doubts, always stay loyal to your heart's callings. You are much stronger than you might think.

The expressive child

The fruit of the union of the dynamic father (number 1) and the kind mother (number 2), the number 3 symbolizes the naïve, happy, and communicative child. See how an open mouth is drawn in its shape, with the glottis in the middle. Much like the majority of children, 3 is spontaneous, sociable, and talkative. Its masculine energy (yang) is strong and dense. It always finds the way to express itself and be noticed. The number 3 resonates with your child self (when you were younger and your inner child was still there), but also with the idea of an entertainer, communicator, and smooth talker. Associated with the natural cycle of birth, life, and death, the number 3 reconnects you to your ability to enjoy each moment and enjoy life fully. Bask in its beautiful and light vibrations. The number 3 spreads happiness all around it, through words, songs, writing, or dancing.

The rigorous worker

With the number 4, there is no shortcut. It is clear, precise, direct, and forthright. Despite the appearances, its feminine energy carries a particularly wise and soft energetic power. Methodical, reliable, stable, and disciplined, this number is connected to born organizers, disciplined people, safeguards, and people who know how to establish boundaries. Solid as a rock, number 4 is a part of life. It's no coincidence if life cycles are made of four seasons (spring, summer, fall, winter), the four stages of life (infancy, youth, middle years, and old age), and the four cardinal points (north, south, east, west). The number 4's mission is to concretely manifest energy in physical structure and matter. Whatever your situation may be when you encounter 4, keep up with the organizational work, honesty, structure, and perseverance.

The curious traveler

The number 5 is aesthetically similar to the number 2, but upside down. Made up of a curve and two lines, it carries a duality that can create a beautiful harmony. Its masculine energy (yang) is rather unusual. The energetic power of the number 5 is particularly strong and dense. What animates the number 5 is going on adventures and discovering the world. A free adventurer, it is ready to clear the way to new paths (physically, psychically, emotionally, intellectually). It is sometimes said that people need to travel or see the world to find themselves from within. This is exactly what the number 5 represents. With it, you constantly seek the balance between your body's desires and your mind's desires. This is why the vibrations of the 5 will take you to the five oceans (Atlantic, Indian, Pacific, Arctic, and Antarctic).

The soft-hearted supervisor

The number 6 is linked to the creation of the world in six days in Genesis. This is why it symbolizes perfection. Visually, it looks like a slightly curved line, drawing a spine behind the stomach of a pregnant woman. Its feminine energy (yin) is particularly wise, tender, and soft. Like a chameleon with many faces, this number represents both man and woman, the family leader, the judge, the lover, or the artist. It's a symbol of creation, fertility, harmony, peace, and healing. It promises you a stable and harmonious home. A warm, kind, and balanced family is essential for this soft number. With it, you will (re)discover with gentleness the power of sharing and helping others and how fulfilling it can be.

The spiritual grandfather

The number 7 is seen as a sacred number. With benevolence, it invites you to climb up your family tree through the lineage of the dynamic father (the number 1). Its masculine energy (yang) is present, but not aggressively so. The energetic power of the number 7 possesses a dense and tranquil strength. In turns, it can be all the faces of knowledge: a professor, philosopher, president, intellectual, priest, or researcher. The number 7 is a reference in terms of knowledge and reflection. Its main purpose is to help your ability to think. Pure, intuitive, and sensitive, this number symbolizes introspection, spirituality, faith, open-mindedness, learning, understanding the world, psychology, magic, and inner wisdom. Be ready: this sacred number invites you on a quest to knowledge.

The powerful strategist

A symbol of infinity, the number 8 is bewitching. Its energy and perpetual quest for balance (from the top to bottom) are literally hypnotic. It is the karmic number of the universal spiritual law of causality, but its energetic power is still soft and wise. Carried by a feminine energy (yin), the number 8 is like an iron fist in a velvet glove. A sharp strategist, it is great at ambitious projects and good at financial and energetic management. Symbolizing the powerful, the hero, and the heroine, the number 8 shares its powerful and large vibrations with most. With it, all things material, career, and business, along with inheritance matters (financial, family, emotional) coming from the feminine lineage (inherited from the kind mother, the number 2), are perfectly dealt with.

The honest altruist

The number 9 perfectly symbolizes the power of accomplishments, for it is the only number that, when multiplied by any other number, can be reduced into itself ($3 \times 9 = 27 = 2 + 7 = 9$).

Carried by the power ending this series of numbers (from 1 to 9), it has the innate ability to end life stages (cycles, relations, work, grief). Its masculine energy (yang) cannot be overlooked. The energetic power of the 9 is particularly strong and dense. Humanitarian in its soul, this number symbolizes the enlightened and upstanding leader, scholar, teacher, tutor, and professor. Its arrival in your life is the confirmation that it is time to move on and act to accomplish your next mission. And this mission implies a greater open-mindedness and consciousness. A symbol of accomplishment, completion, and plenitude in your gifts, the number 9 represents the perfection of your ideas through to the three divine manifestations (over three planes: soul, mind, and body).

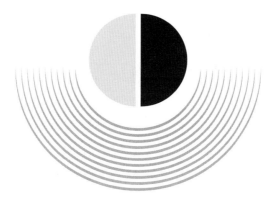

MASTER NUMBERS

The master numbers are the numbers 11, 22, and 33. In numerology, they are also called enhanced or particular numbers. Each master number brings a strong vibratory force that doubles the power of the number 1, 2, or 3. It also amplifies the energy of the number 2 through the number 11 ($1 + 1 = 2$), of the number 4 through the number 22 ($2 + 2 = 4$), and of the number 6 through the number 33 ($3 + 3 = 6$).

The atypical spiritual guide

I invite you to read the symbolism of numbers 1 and 2 before reading the symbolic of number 11. This master number carries a particularly strong and intense magnetic energy. It is said to be an inspired leader, a channel for divination, a super-guide, a super-teacher, a super-messenger, and the "most" part of ourselves. Number 11 is a true "main character." A symbol of the link between the sky and the earth but also of self-discovery, the moon, and fertility, this master number will help you fully embody yourself if you're interacting with other people.

When alone and cut off from the world, this luminous 11 will falter and quickly carry you towards a maze of frustration and dependency. When you encounter this number, remember to cultivate your creative power by accumulating collaborations, teamwork, and interactions.

The ambitious builder

Read the symbolism of the numbers 2 and 4 before reading about the number 22. This master number possesses an unusually remarkable building energy. Its strong and dense masculine energy (yang) doesn't go unnoticed. The number 22 has a universal ambition and an incredible determination that can take him far. You will also find it at the origin of the greatest realizations and most important constructions. It is not by chance that it took twenty-two basic elements to create the world. As a visionary and intuitive builder, this master number represents the super-humanitarian maker. It is an unparalleled master builder and is very experienced. Let its unfaltering determination carry you. The number 22 knows what it wants and will help you do everything it takes to achieve it. With it, almost nothing can stop you!

33

The devoted instructor

I advise you to read the symbolism of the numbers 3 and 6 before reading about the number 33. This master number possesses a very influential energy. Its power is particularly remarkable, strong, and intense. It is said to be a super-guide (see master number 11) mixed with a super-humanitarian maker (see master number 22). In a nutshell, 33 is a master teacher and universal guide. Through it, the superior power, the enlightened triangle (the addition of 11 and 22), humanity, family, harmony, and innovation are transcended and expressed. If you cross paths with a number 33, then it is time to turn to the world. The only priority of this master number is to bring its help to others in other to relieve their pain.

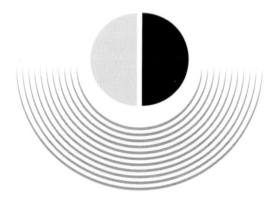

ELEMENTS AND NUMEROLOGY

As you have just discovered, each number possesses a strong symbolism. To go further in the exploration of intuitive numerology, I invite you to discover the power of the four elements. Earth, water, air, or fire? Which elements are you the closest to? To find out, answer the next page's test.

TEST YOURSELF!

Take a deep breath and calmly read the following affirmations. In complete honesty and transparency with yourself, select the sentences that apply to you. Analyze your answers thanks to the correspondences chart and discover your element. Let's go!

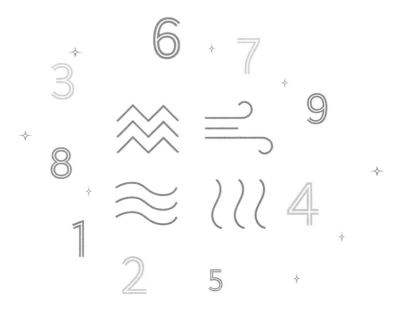

The elements test

☐ **1.** I am ambitious, passionate, and brave.

☐ **2.** People say I have a gentle strength.

☐ **3.** I am scared of heights, and I don't like extreme sports.

☐ **4.** My favorite number is 2, 7, or 22.

☐ **5.** People say I can be intuitive and spiritual, but also frivolous and casual.

☐ **6.** I am rational and have always been down-to-earth.

☐ **7.** The historical figure that I associate with the most is the warrior.

☐ **8.** I believe in the power of abundance and in the law of attraction.

☐ **9.** My favorite number is 5 or 6.

☐ **10.** I easily take on a maternal role (within a family or a group).

☐ **11.** I am a soft with a slow but fluid rhythm.

☐ **12.** I am open-minded, instinctive, and open to new things.

☐ **13.** My favorite number is 4 or 8.

☐ **14.** My main values are freedom and peace.

☐ **15.** When I am emotionally unstable, I slowly burn myself out.

☐ **16.** I like harmony, clarity, consistency, and balance.

☐ **17.** My favorite number is 1, 3, 9, 11, or 33.

☐ **18.** I am a great confidant when I can control my emotions.

☐ **19.** I am very creative, and I have a lot of energy.

☐ **20.** I like traveling, because it represents discoveries and being in motion.

> **LIST THE CHECKED SENTENCES HERE:** ....

Compare your results to the chart on page 117.
Your element is the one with which you have the most numbers in common.

RESULTS

EARTH	WATER	AIR	FIRE
3, 6, 8, 10, 13	2, 4, 11, 16, 18	5, 9, 12, 14, 20	1, 7, 15, 17, 19

Your element is
EARTH

Earth's keywords are realism, sturdiness, organization, determination, stability, the quiet, and the tangible. Like a tree taking root, Mother Nature is a symbol of abundance, fertility, creation, and maternity. Your second nature is to take care and nourish others. People ruled by the element earth are very methodical and precise; they act without rushing. They need comfort and tranquility to appease their materialistic tendencies. Generally receptive and discreet, they want to do well and are hardworking, which helps them achieve their goals. Their combativeness and rigor can make them harsh, strict, introverted, and inflexible. Because they lack fantasy, whimsy, and imagination, down-to-earth and rational people can sometimes be called "buzzkills"

Your lucky numbers are 4 and 8
The number 4 is direct and forthright. Visually, it is made of only three straight lines.

The number 8 is the karmic and spiritual number of the causal link. The energy of this number lies in actions and direct consequences.

Your element is
WATER

Water's keywords are emotions, softness, consistency, regeneration, harmony, balance, clearness, and reverie. Equipped with a gentle and profound strength, it allows you to accept and avoid obstacles to get what you want. This rare ability is a true asset in our current society, which is always so fast-paced. People ruled by water can slow down this rhythm, which can sometimes drag us too quickly through our day-to-day obligations and commitments (work, family, hobbies, friends). Their soft wisdom and collected balance are beneficial for most people.

Intuitive and sensitive, you can be overwhelmed by contradictory emotions and feelings. You then become hard to grasp, dependent, and influenced by how others perceive you. Try to not let big changes upset you, even if they disturb your need for stability.

Your lucky numbers are 2, 7, and 22
Between its straight line and its curve, the number 2 knows how to use its great inner duality. A sacred number, the number 7 is the archetype of the kind grandfather. The master number 22 brings a strong vibration that doubles the power of the number 2.

Your element is

AIR

Air's keywords are evasion, casualness, extroversion, action, motion, openness, spirituality, intuition, and freedom. People ruled by air are curious, amiable, and easily adaptable. However, if their need to express themselves is not met, they may get lost in their own thoughts by isolating themselves. They first instinct is still to discover new things (cultures, countries, people, experiences, environments).

Instinctively peaceful, they impulsively follow their whims. Sometimes frivolous and casual (in the wrong way), these people can struggle to achieve their goals. Their tendency to be versatile can trap them in a vicious circle of doubt, fear, and procrastination.

Your lucky numbers are 5 and 6
The number 5 is the fourth prime number. It is made of two duos: $1 + 4$ and $2 + 3$.

By referencing the creation of the world in six days in Genesis, the number 6 represents perfection.

Your element is

FIRE

Fire's keywords are energy, boldness, ambition, bravery, determination, tenacity, courage, and strength. People ruled by fire have a strong impulsivity and an unmatched passion. Their energy and originality inspire them to put colors in other people's lives. Equipped with a rare honesty, a childish spontaneity, and a brutal bluntness, they can sometimes be hurtful. Whenever these people cross your path (whether it be for a minute, a month, or a decade), they leave a mark, either good or bad. They are creative people who excessively love life. Exuberant, confident, proud, and explosive, they can incarnate an incredible source of motivation, enthusiasm, or destruction. It all depends on what they decide to do.

Your lucky numbers are 1, 3, 9, 11, and 33

The number 1 is the father of all numbers. Its energetic power is strong and dense. With a yang energy (masculine) like number 1, number 3 is the expressive and joyful child, traditionally the fruit of the union of the father (number 1) and the mother (number 2).

The number 9 is the perfect symbol of the power of accomplishments. It's the only number that, when multiplied by any other number, is reduced to itself.

The numbers 11 and 33 are special, for they are part of the master numbers. They bring a strong vibration that doubles the power of a number (1 for 11, 3 for 33).

WHAT IS A LUCKY NUMBER?

Lucky numbers are numbers that are especially favorable for you. Generally speaking, they promise good luck and good surprises. Your numbers' vibrations are familiar to you; I invite you to exploit their benefits to their maximum by reading about their symbolism (pp. 117–119).

✦

SIMILAR RESULTS

If you have an equal result for different elements, it means your sensitivity is higher than average. You will thus have more lucky numbers to explore!

✦

NUMBER RECURRENCE

Compare your element's lucky numbers with the numbers that often cross your path, but also the results of all the calculations you have made in the third part of this book. The more they are repeated, the more these numbers will have a particular importance in your life.

DEVELOP YOUR

ELEMENT'S ENERGY

Use intuitive numerology and the elements' symbolism as personal development tools. In order to bask in the energy of your main elements (and the lucky numbers associated to it), I invite you to explore it first. Then, to balance out yourself entirely, explore the others one by one.

EARTH

Your goal is grounding

To ground yourself more and reinforce your energetic base, I advise you to solidify your anchors. The goal is to leave the left hemisphere of your brain and move toward your gut, in order to become fully conscious of your body and feel safe within it. Feeling grounded also means accepting your body so that you can calmly commit in life. In order to do so, practice the grounding meditation (p. 123), walk barefoot whenever you can and focus on the feeling of your feet on the ground, wear red or brown clothes, carry red or brown lithotherapy stones (jasper, fossilized wood, bullseye, etc.), cook fresh produce that grows in the ground (konjac root, potatoes, carrots, etc.), and most importantly, laugh without moderation.

Little by little, leave your comfort zone by bringing imagination and fantasy to your daily life. Try a new meal, a new outing, or an unusual activity, or visit an unknown place.

WATER

Your goal is independence

The more you cultivate your autonomy and keep your goals in mind, the more you will extinguish the burning bushes of our society (negativity, violence, precariousness, oppression, etc.). Your power lies in your personal flow of softness and serenity. To preserve it, savor the moment by taking your time and doing things at your pace. Some advice: you should never doubt your values or what makes your heart flutter. From the earliest age, we carry the weight and glances of society. With time, these things can impact you negatively. Slowly but surely, this will gnaw on your self-esteem. Cherish and respect the three pillars of self-esteem:

- Loving yourself
- The correct image of what you represent
- Believing in what you achieve

Being confident and trusting your uniqueness means being carried by the belief that you will succeed and that you will accomplish beautiful things. Just like water runs day and night, you will act without fear of failure or judgment every day of the year, without interruption.

AIR

Your goal is realizing your dreams

Wanting to do a lot of things and to have many amazing experiences is good, but it's not the same as actually doing them. If you wish to go beyond your dreams by actually accomplishing them, here is my advice in two parts.

First, pick one goal at a time. It should be positive and focused on the near future, and it must contain a subject and a verb (conjugated in the present). For instance: I travel to Quebec.

Second, your goal must be all of the following:

- Personal. It relies on you entirely, and only you are responsible for it 100 percent.

- Simple. A ten-year-old should be able to understand it.

- Realistic. You must be able to accomplish it; it must be achievable.

- Ambitious. To reach it, you must make an effort (but the goal shouldn't be insurmountable).

- Measurable. Your goal should be factual and dated. For example: I will travel to Quebec in the fall of 2025.

- Positive. Your goal should be good for you but also for your loved ones.

FIRE

Your goal is refocusing yourself

When agitation takes over and hurts your mental health, emotions, and physical health, use the following exercise. When a situation is complicated, and you're faced with an unsettling challenge or a relational crisis, ask yourself this immediately, while being as objective as possible: will this still matter in five hours, five days, five months, or five years? According to your answer, put things in perspective and allow yourself five minutes to cool down. Don't do things halfway; really express your frustration by hitting a pillow or by screaming as loud as you can alone in a room.

You are filled with an incredible and powerful energy. Allow it to flow within you by getting a massage once a month, exercising daily (walking, running, dancing, team sports), or by using a grounding technique of your choice (meditation, gardening, pottery, cooking).

MY GROUNDING
MEDITATION

Sit down on a chair, but don't lean against its back and don't cross your legs. Put your bare feet against the ground, and place the palms of your hands against your thighs. Relax, close your eyes, and pay attention to your breathing.

Then, in your own rhythm, focus on your stomach, your hips, and your legs, and imagine that tall and long roots are growing from your feet. They reach deep into the ground to go to the center of the earth. There, you collect as much luminous energy as you can before carrying this energy back to the top of your skull. While you are rooted, a thread comes out of your head and reaches over the clouds to go higher and higher into the Universe, where it stays hooked. Here, you are grounded. What are your sensations? How are you feeling? Pay attention to the emotions you are feeling. Give shape to the positive ones by visualizing them as a dot of light that is nestled deep within your heart. Your roots will be invisible, but you can connect yourself to them at all times thanks to this anchor.

COLORS AND NUMEROLOGY

✦

Continue your journey into the heart of intuitive numerology by discovering the power of colors. Each number vibrates and emits an energy of its own. It is the same for colors. That is why some numbers have the same vibratory frequency as certain colors. Red, green, blue-purple, or yellow-orange? Which color feels the closest to you? To find out, I'm inviting you to answer the test next page.

TEST YOURSELF!

Like with all the other tests, ground yourself and calmly read the following affirmations. Select the ones that correspond with you. Analyze your answers thanks to the correspondence charts. Then discover your color. Let's go!

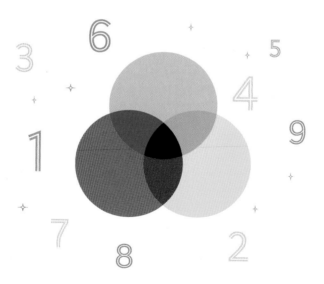

The colors test:

- ☐ **1.** I am very ambitious, motivated, passionate, and brave.
- ☐ **2.** I have a discreet nature, and I rarely chose to speak up and reveal myself.
- ☐ **3.** I relieve the stress of others.
- ☐ **4.** My favorite number is 5, 6, or 7.
- ☐ **5.** I am said to be dynamic, creative, radiant, and optimistic.
- ☐ **6.** I like quietness and the relaxation one feels in the woods or the countryside.
- ☐ **7.** I like to create and take action to accomplish my biggest dreams.
- ☐ **8.** I believe in self-healing and luck.
- ☐ **9.** My favorite number is 2, 3, 22, or 33.
- ☐ **10.** I am a victim of energy vampires who absorb all my energy.
- ☐ **11.** I am a secretive, calm, peaceful, and spiritual person.
- ☐ **12.** I like to help communications and relations run smoothly.
- ☐ **13.** I am an excellent confidant and adviser because I possess a great intuition.
- ☐ **14.** People sometimes think I'm too childish because I don't take myself seriously and I'm carefree.
- ☐ **15.** When I'm not happy about something, I can quickly be irritated and upset.
- ☐ **16.** People say I'm melancholic, elusive, and volatile.
- ☐ **17.** My favorite number is 1, 8, 9, or 11.
- ☐ **18.** My favorite number is 4.
- ☐ **19.** People say I'm charismatic, and I don't go unnoticed.
- ☐ **20.** As a sunny person, I can sometimes be too self-absorbed and proud.

> ### LIST THE CHECKED SENTENCES HERE: ....

Compare your results to the chart on page 126.
Your corresponding color is the one with which you have the most numbers in common.

RESULTS

RED	BLUE-PURPLE	YELLOW-ORANGE	GREEN
1, 7, 15, 17, 19	22, 4, 11, 16, 13	5, 9, 12, 14, 20	3, 6, 8, 10, 18

Your color is

RED

The keywords for red are power, boldness, bravery, determination, charisma, passion, excess, intensity, and authority.

It is the warmest and strongest color in the light spectrum, and red was the first name attributed to a color. It seems to be the first chromatic nuance we can perceive as babies. Red is striking and unconsciously embedded inside us all. Simply magical, red is the color with the most impact on our physiological functions. No need to up the thermostat, for this color naturally warms up a room, both visually and physically.

With this intense color, there is no middle ground. Red is as energizing as it is dangerous. The silent force of the ambitious leader, it is particularly aphrodisiac. It arouses desire and excites the senses.

Your lucky numbers are 1, 8, 9, and 11

The master number 11 symbolizes bright red. It is intense, and it doubles the power of the number 1.

The number 1 possesses an energetic vibration that is strong, dense, and remarkable.

The number 8 is a builder, a sharp strategist, and an ambitious and powerful being. It is the true hero.

Being the only number that is reduced to itself when multiplied, 9 represents the enlightened and honest leader.

Your color is

BLUE-PURPLE

The keywords for blue-purple are peace of mind, serenity, transcendence, mystery, discretion, aloofness, solemnity, and seriousness.

Spirituality is indeed very important for blue-purple, for it symbolizes religious fervor and divine inspiration. For Catholics, blue represents the Virgin Mary, and for Hindus, it represents the divinities Vishnu and Krishna (one of the incarnations of Vishnu), who have blue skin. As for purple, it is a great catalyst to (re)connect with your unconscious. It is not rare to see purple on Catholic bishops' outfits or in the offices of therapists who practice hypnosis (or any other introspection or energetic technique). The flip side of blue is that when used too much, it can lead to lethargic, dull, or depressive states where one could feel melancholic, negative, and defeated. During the Middle Ages, purple was called "subniger" meaning "half-mourning," which makes it a color associated with mourning (more exactly, the period of time after a year of mourning, when someone could wear purple instead of black). It's usually rejected, misunderstood, and disliked by children and seen as too vulgar in the collective unconscious. Too ambivalent, too hard to grasp, and too versatile, purple is rarely in the top three of the most loved colors.

Your lucky numbers are 5, 6, and 7
The numbers 5 and 6 refer to the color blue. The number 5 represents the free thinker and the adventurer, ready to clear the way toward new paths (intellectually, psychically, or physically).

The number 6 particularly resonates with the color indigo. It symbolizes acceptance, idealism, harmony, peace, and healing.

The sacred number 7 is associated with purple. It represents knowledge (the philosopher, the researcher, the professor, the priest) and the mastery of knowledge and thinking.

Your color is
YELLOW-ORANGE

The keywords for yellow-orange are dynamism, radiance, abundance, fulfillment, optimism, communication, and open-mindedness. Thanks to yellow, you are basking in your success. Thanks to its vibrations, you attract sympathy, attention, and happiness. Yellow makes your life as soft as honey. A symbol of parties and friendship, yellow is a true and natural boost of energy. No other color can rival its dynamism and vitality.

Linked to the left hemisphere of the brain, yellow helps you assimilate new ideas and concepts, and helps open your mind so you can understand things more easily. Thanks to the color yellow, we become more vibrant and charismatic—but watch out for excesses of ego. Yellow should light things up, not blind or burn them.

Orange is the color of constant metamorphosis and evolution. It possesses a serene and controlled power. As the color of technology, communication, and sharing, orange sparkles like a beautiful bonfire around which we all dance.

Your lucky numbers are 2, 3, 22, and 33

The numbers 3 and 33 vibrate with yellow. The number 3 represents the child (the one you were as a kid but also your inner child, always here) and the communicator. The master number 33 is associated with the triangle, enlightenment, and creative innovation. The numbers 2 and 22 are closer to orange. The number 2 symbolizes the feminine part of the self, the sensitive man, the dependent, and the adviser. The master number 22 represents the master, visionary, and humanitarian builder.

Your color is

GREEN

The keywords for green are vital energy, patience, antistress, health growth stability, ecology, ephemeral, misfortune, and hope. Green appeases and calms. It naturally lowers blood pressure. The chosen color in the medical world, the color green naturally possesses interesting therapeutic properties. It comforts, calms agitated minds, balances your nervous system, and deeply revitalizes all your energies. Like an actual

breath of fresh air, this color invites you in its generous and vegetal bubble, as light as it is happy. But green clears up the mind, and its clarity can be brutal and sharp if one isn't ready for it.

Your lucky number is 4

The number 4 is associated with balance, stability, methodology, family, and life's natural cycles. Think of the four seasons, the four cardinal points, and the four stages of life (infancy, youth, the middle years, and old age).

SIMILAR RESULTS If you have an equal result for different colors, it means your sensitivity is higher than average. You will thus have more lucky numbers to explore!

MAXIMIZE THE POWER OF

YOUR COLOR

Use intuitive numerology and color symbolism as self-development tools. To bask in the energy of your main color (and the lucky numbers associated with it), I invite you to read about it first. Then, in order to holistically balance your mind, read about the other colors, one by one.

RED

Your goal is the full awareness of your body

To lower the emotions in your body and strengthen your energetic base, here are four things to try in your every-day life:

- Walk and dance barefoot as often as you can, while focusing on the feeling of your feet on the ground.

- Wear red or brown clothes, or carry red or brown lithotherapy stones (jasper, fossilized wood, bullseye, etc.).

- Cook fresh produce that grows in the ground (konjac root, potatoes, carrots, etc.).

- Little by little, widen your comfort zone with imagination and whimsy. For example, go dancing, try a new activity, or visit a place you've never seen before.

BLUE-PURPLE

Your goal is to be more positive

I truly believe in these words of Oprah Winfrey: "The greatest discovery of all time is that a person can change his future by merely changing his attitude." And as many studies have shown it, about half of our happiness only relies on ourselves. Thus, you truly are the co-builder of your life!

To chase the negative thoughts as soon as they arrive, I invite you to try this simple and fun exercise. Write down what happiness means to you. Write your definition of happiness as a starting point, and then allow the ideas associated with it to flow. Let your intuition run wild without shame or fear. Then, organize your ideas into four big categories:

- Pleasures (the joy you feel).

- Commitment (the activities that mean something to you).

- Satisfaction (the satisfaction of what you have accomplished).

- Serenity (the perspective you have on things).

Explore, contemplate, and deal with the four aspects of your happiness in depth. Which category deserves to be acted upon right now?

YELLOW-ORANGE

Your goal is to shine

To cultivate your communicative energy, I advise you to do a digital light detox. Instead of sitting pointlessly in front of your computer or smartphone, try a cure of light therapy. Switch the blue light (big disruptor of your sleep and vision) with a light closer to sunlight. Natural light activates your positive stress hormone, cortisol.

GREEN

Your goal is to be Zen

To preserve your calm attitude, I invite you to try the energetic concept of the forest bath (sylvotherapy). As simple as it seems, this natural method has a great effect on the body (it lowers cortisol levels and stress hormones, slows the heartbeat, and lowers blood pressure and glycemic index). Not unlike meditation, sylvotherapy allows you to reconnect with nature, the environment, and your true self by developing all your senses.

While you're walking in the woods, your garden, or a park, hug the trees! Whether you're trying this alone or with your kids, open your senses and let go. Let the tree envelop you with its beautiful and revitalizing energy. However, avoid practicing sylvotherapy with exotic or decorative trees, as they can be toxic.

BOOST YOUR ENERGY
- When you wake up, help your energy circulate by rubbing your hands together. Place them on your heart or your solar plexus, and observe the effect it has. What are you feeling?
- Yawn and stretch! Yawning reoxygenates your brain, and stretching gets your blood flowing.

ANIMALS AND NUMEROLOGY

✦

Continue your journey by exploring an intuitive numerology symbolism that can be quite original: animal symbolism. Discover the intimate connection between numerology and animals. Fish, reptile, bird, or wild animal? Which animal feels closest to you? To find out, fill out the test on the next page.

TEST YOURSELF!

Ground yourself and select the affirmations that correspond with you. Analyze your answers according to the correspondence charts. Then discover your animal. Let's go!

The animal test:

☐ **1.** Independence and freedom are very important to me.

☐ **2.** As a great and charismatic protector, I instinctively defend those I love.

☐ **3.** I feel particularly comfortable in the water.

☐ **4.** My favorite number is 1, 7, or 8.

☐ **5.** People say that I am trustworthy because I am always down-to-earth.

☐ **6.** I like to dive deep, whether it's agreeable or painful.

☐ **7.** I associate with the archetype of the adventurer.

☐ **8.** I am perpetually transitioning.

☐ **9.** My favorite numbers are 3 and 9.

☐ **10.** I regularly remember my dreams, and they are often premonitory.

☐ **11.** I am a quick, spontaneous, impatient, and intense person.

☐ **12.** I prefer to stay discreet, for I am quickly overwhelmed by my dark and light sides.

☐ **13.** My favorite numbers are 5 and 7.

☐ **14.** My main values are metamorphosis, adaptability, and integrity.

☐ **15.** I tend to run from my responsibilities.

☐ **16.** I fear almost nothing.

☐ **17.** My favorite number is 2, 4, 6, or 8.

☐ **18.** When I have an idea in mind, I can't let it go!

☐ **19.** I am very creative and have a lot of energy.

☐ **20.** I know how to walk a lonely road, slowly but surely.

> ## LIST THE CHECKED SENTENCES HERE: ....

Compare your results to the chart on page 133.

Your corresponding animal is the one with which you have the most numbers in common.

RESULTS

BIRD	WILD ANIMAL	REPTILE	FISH
1, 7, 15, 17, 19	2, 4, 11, 16, 18	5, 9, 12, 14, 20	3, 6, 8, 10, 13

Your animal is

THE BIRD

The keywords of the bird are freedom, motion, independence, flight, life power, fertility, luck, fluidity, casualness, and dream.

The people associated with the bird can quickly stand on their own two feet to always go higher and farther. These bold and independent personalities can reach the highest spheres of society, like highly coveted jobs and generally envied situations. However, as soon as they feel their freedom slipping away, they tend to flee their responsibilities. Any limitation will restrict them, like a wild bird put in a cage.

Your lucky numbers are 2, 4, 6, and 8

With its curve and straight line, the number 2 represents a great duality. It's not a coincidence that a swan looks like a 2. This is a free yet loyal and faithful animal.

The number 4 represents the natural cycles of life: the four seasons, the four cardinal points, the four stages of life (infancy, youth, the middle years, and old age).

The number 6 symbolizes peace, idealism, harmony, and healing.

The number 8 is the infinity number. Its energy, oscillating from top to bottom, is bewitching and hypnotic.

Your animal is

THE WILD ANIMAL

The keywords of the wild animal are bravery, liveliness, dynamism, energy, natural, rapidity, versatility, authoritarianism, and dissimulation.

Within every domesticated animal, there is the heart of a wild animal. Untamed and unpredictable, the wild animal seemingly has no limits. Following the cycles of seasons and the lives of its peers, it develops an outstanding adaptability. People often say that creativity is born from constraints. In the wild, felines have understood this very well, for they always get their way. They are ready to do almost anything to be respected. The powerful lion roars whenever it wants, while the panther watches over its territory from up high. The tiger is not less authoritarian; it imposes its rules and doesn't hesitate to change them at will.

Your lucky numbers are 1, 7, and 8

The number 1 possesses a yang (masculine) energy. It is the father of all numbers. Its power is strong and dense.

The sacred number 7 invites you into the genealogy of the father's lineage (the number 1).

The number 8 is a strong number, which energy resides in actions and the direct consequences of those actions.

Your animal is
THE REPTILE

The keywords of the reptile are transmutation, metamorphosis, rebirth, letting go, perseverance, stamina, stubbornness, cunning, and deceit.

A main character in many myths and legends, the snake is the king of change. The shedding of the snake,

lizard, turtle, or crocodile is the finest proof. The people ruled by the energy of the reptile are discreet but always accomplish their goals. Their greatest challenge is probably welcoming and taming their imperfections along with their other qualities and flaws.

Your lucky numbers are 3 and 9

The number 3 represents the natural cycle (birth, life, death), rebirth, and protection.

The number 9 symbolizes human immortality in Freemasonry. Egyptians gave this name to the sacred mountain of the sun because for them (just like the Greeks), this number is sacred.

Your animal is
THE FISH

The keywords of the fish are dynamism, motion, change, fertility, luck, wisdom, introspection, and mysticism.

The fish can be found in many cultures and religions. A symbol of Christianity and different Hindu deities, and the Buddhist symbol for happiness, the fish is a guide through many journeys and is turned toward others. If your animal is the fish, you have intuitive knowledge and sharp intelligence. Staying at the surface superficially doesn't interest you. You like to dive deep. Like the fish that always keeps its eyes open, your potential is awakened and you have the innate ability to help other awaken their potential.

Your lucky numbers are 5 and 7
The number 5 symbolizes energy (physical, intellectual, sexual), freedom, versatility, and the five oceans (Atlantic, Indian, Pacific, Arctic, and Antarctic).

The number 7 is a sacred number. It represents learning, understanding the world, magic, and accomplishing one's inner wisdom.

SIMILAR RESULTS If you have an equal result for different animals, it means your sensitivity is higher than average. You will thus have more lucky numbers to explore!

NOURISH YOUR ANIMAL ENERGY

Use intuitive numerology and animal symbolism as self-development tools. To bask in the energy of your main animal (and the lucky numbers associated with it), I invite you to read about it first. Then, in order to holistically balance your mind, read about the other animals, one by one.

BIRD

Your goal is to be responsible

Have you ever wondered what responsibility truly is? Today, being responsible means looking a certain way that is acceptable in the eyes of others and society. It's about conforming to outside expectations and precise rules in order to receive the approbation of others. The validation of our degree of responsibility then comes from the outside and leads to a sense of security through this approval. And yet, I believe that we are all responsible for the results we obtain. It is absolutely unfair to blame others or our life's circumstances, for it is we who hold the reins of our life. We are the main cause of our happiness, success, joys, or misfortune. Responsibility doesn't mean the deprivation of freedom. On the contrary! To fully take responsibility for yourself means being committed to yourself and respecting your own values. If your animal is the bird, it means one of your values is freedom. You can then be responsible and free.

WILD ANIMAL

Your goal is quietness (internal and external)

Do your liveliness and your passionate reactions sometimes cause you trouble? To appease your anger, I advise you to reduce your sources of frustration and discontent. Identify the things in your life that are making you outraged, disappointed, impatient, and even angry. What can you do to stop encouraging these things? It may sound blunt and direct, but I often tell my consultants that a job can be quit; that we can leave an unsatisfying relationship; that experiences, studies, or dreams can be accomplished; and that money can both be attracted and lost. If you don't change the way you do things or your situation, it means you find it fulfilling somehow (even unconsciously).

Unless you're a masochist, you derive no pleasure from being angry. It destroys more than it nourishes (liver issues, digestive problems, skin problems, etc.). Try to practice meditation, relaxation, or brief therapies like Emotional Freedom Techniques (better known as EFT).

FISH

Your goal is to help without saving

Because you possess the innate ability to help others awaken their personal potential, remember that helping is not saving. Otherwise, you might quickly get lost in the Bermuda Triangle of psychology. In transactional analysis, this triangle is named the Karpman drama triangle, after its creator.

Even if the role of savior can be very rewarding for your ego, it turns you into a falsely obliging person. Indeed, you end game is actually to keep people under your thumb by making them incapable of dealing with things on their own. Despite the greatest compassion, the purest love, or the best intentions in the world, you cannot erase someone else's challenges. They must face them themselves and learn life lessons from them, no matter how hard. It is counterproductive to take away from someone the possibility to live their own experiences that could help them develop their bravery, tenacity, creativity, or patience. By saving them, you cut the bird's wings so it can't fly, and you do not respect the experience it could gather from falling from the nest, for example. When someone is facing difficulties, listen to them, but before acting on their behalf, ask yourself if your interlocutor really needs your help. If yes, how? Then, ask yourself: Are you the best person to help them? What are the boundaries you need to set? By helping this person, are you respecting your needs and well-being?

REPTILE

Your goal is to accept that you are imperfect

For a long time I believed that unveiling my imperfections was a sign of weakness. This limiting belief fed my very well-oiled self-sabotage. Even if it takes time and effort, I believe it is never too late to bid perfectionism farewell. Wabi sabi could help. This Japanese expression from the 15th century is derived from wabi, meaning melancholy, loveliness, sadness, or simplicity, and sabi, which represents the alteration of time, the patina of time on old objects, decrepitude, or the taste for old things. Wabi sabi is an aesthetic concept derived from Zen and Taoist principles. The Japanese art of kintsugi, which consists of repairing and adorning the cracks in an object with gold, is a perfect example of wabi sabi. As if you were a beautiful chawan (an ancient bowl for tea), cover your scars with gold and embrace your imperfections. It will help you better tame and accept them. You will then strengthen your self-confidence and develop new skills to face the challenges life will throw at you.

THE KARPMAN DRAMA TRIANGLE
Created in 1968 and named after its creator, this diagram describes a basic relational scenario between a victim, a persecutor, and a rescuer. It is a mirror of the unhealthy manipulation that can arise from two people's interactions, and it demonstrates that one can alternate all three roles. Every time we struggle to express our ideas, feelings, or emotions, we unconsciously carry one of these three roles, thus disturbing our relationships and how we communicate.

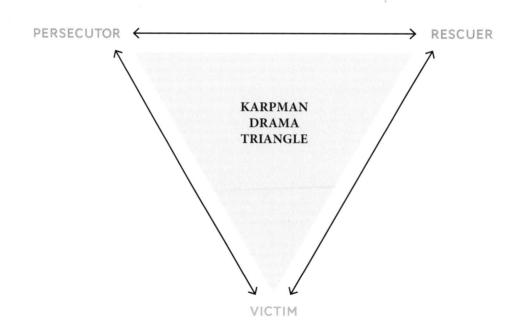

PERSECUTOR ← → RESCUER

KARPMAN
DRAMA
TRIANGLE

VICTIM

PERSONALITIES AND NUMEROLOGY

✦

Continue your journey into the symbolism of intuitive numerology with the different personality types. Discover the connection that unites numerology to these character traits. Extrovert, thinker, leader, or planner? Which role instinctively corresponds to you the most? To discover it, fill out the test next page.

TEST YOURSELF!

By now, you know how this works. In complete honesty and transparency with yourself, select the sentences that apply to you. Analyze your answers thanks to the correspondences chart. Then, discover your personality. Let's go!

The personality test:

- ☐ **1.** I like to plan, coordinate, and build (projects, relationships, etc.).
- ☐ **2.** People always call me when there's a conflict or a fight within a group.
- ☐ **3.** People say I'm a relentless motivator, but that I can be annoying!
- ☐ **4.** My favorite number is 2, 3, or 5.
- ☐ **5.** I like to meditate and take the time for deep thinking and introspection.
- ☐ **6.** I instinctively take the lead in projects, groups, and relationships.
- ☐ **7.** I don't like ideas and concepts that aren't tangible and efficient.
- ☐ **8.** I struggle to listen others and let them express their ideas.
- ☐ **9.** My favorite number is 7, 9, or 33.
- ☐ **10.** Everything I create finds its audience and is supported by others.
- ☐ **11.** I like to share, laugh, and talk with a friend or a large group.
- ☐ **12.** I easily take on the role of the wise leader or the eldest (in a family or a group)
- ☐ **13.** My favorite number is 1, 8, or 11.
- ☐ **14.** People sometimes think I'm too indoorsy, solitary, or "in my own little bubble."
- ☐ **15.** I am independent, tidy, and strict.
- ☐ **16.** I'm always the first to party in my group of friends or my family.
- ☐ **17.** My favorite numbers are 4, 6, and 22.
- ☐ **18.** Whenever I'm alone for too long, loneliness weighs on me.
- ☐ **19.** I struggle to accept criticism, especially when people aren't following my plans.
- ☐ **20.** My main values are free thinking and intellectualization.

> ## LIST THE CHECKED SENTENCES HERE: ....

Compare your results to the chart on page 141.
Your corresponding personality is the one with which you have the most numbers in common.

RESULTS

PLANNER	SOCIABLE	THINKER	LEADER
1, 7, 15, 17, 19	2, 4, 11, 16, 18	5, 9, 12, 14, 20	3, 6, 8, 10, 13

You are
THE PLANNER

The keywords of the planner are rationality, rigor, detail, planning, demanding nature, intolerance, and perfectionism.

Efficient and productive, you don't waste time in seeing your projects through and accomplishing your goals. You are patient and committed, you know how to deal with the unexpected, and stress has almost no effect on you. Foresight and adaptability are some of your finest qualities. Whatever happens in your life, you are like a Swiss army knife: always with a plan A, B, or even C.

Your lucky numbers are 4, 6, and 22
The roles of the number 4 are the reliable and organized worker, the disciplined person, the builder of solid foundations, the safeguard, and the one who sets boundaries.

The number 6, however, represents the responsible person, the representative of justice, and the head of the family, the patriarch.

As a master number, 22 is a visionary builder, a project manager, an ambitious and amazing maker.

You are
THE SOCIABLE

They keywords of the sociable are open-mindedness, empathy, active listening, emotional intelligence, communication, mediation, and emotional dependency.

The sociable personality is comfortable in public. You naturally know how to listen, converse, and talk about various subjects. You're the life of the party and love to be surrounded in order to live strong and intense collective moments with others (family reunions, gatherings, concerts, travels, etc.). However, whenever you are alone, you feel submerged by loneliness, and it can affect your beautiful energy.

Your lucky numbers are 2, 3, and 5
The number 2 possesses great relational abilities. It is at ease when it comes to collaboration, and it easily evolves in teams,

at work, at sports events, or in a family. With a sociable and accommodating nature, the number 2 is a good mediator.

The roles of the number 3 are the communicator, the host, and the smooth talker.

The life of number 5 is a series of experiences to be lived fully. Very curious and willing, it has hobbies and passions that suit it, and it favors self-expression and diversity.

president, priest, researcher, etc.), the reference in knowledge and reflection, the thinking side of the self, and the radiant guide.

The 9 represents erudition, altruism, and humanitarianism, for it is an enlightened and honest leader.

The master number 33 is a master teacher, combining the energies of the super-guide (number 11) and the master builder (number 22).

You are
THE THINKER

The keywords of the thinker are reflection, introspection, meditation, focus, prudence, sedentary lifestyle, self-exclusion, and misanthropy.

Improvisation has no place in your daily life. Every time you take action, it is upon lengthy reflection. You rely on your intelligence a lot, and you are right! You possess a rare ability for dealing with subjects in depth, for many hours. While others get bored quickly, it's not rare to see you get swept away by the story of a novel or the discovery of a new subject. Loyal to the logic of your left brain, you never leave anything to chance and never act rashly, in fear of making a mistake.

Your lucky numbers are 7, 9, and 33
The roles of the sacred number 7 are the professionals of knowledge (philosopher,

You are
THE LEADER

The keywords of the leader are leadership, strength, determination, self-assertion, boldness, dynamism, self-confidence, intolerance, and pretentiousness.

The leader is an unmatched motivator. Your ability to carry others and to drag and push them toward their desired goals is incredible. Even when you don't always have the corresponding professional status, you are a born leader. Brave and combative, you are bursting with energy. You take matters into your own hands almost all the time. But be careful not to force your way of thinking onto others. Otherwise, your great power could turn against you.

Your lucky numbers are 1, 8, and 11
The number 1 is the same number that can be written the same way in all the

languages, in the shape of a staff, one straight vertical line.

The number 8 symbolizes power, strategy, management (of energy and finances), ambition, and heroism.

The master number 11 possesses a particularly intense energetic power. It is often said to be magnetic.

SIMILAR RESULTS If you have an equal result for different personalities, it means your sensitivity is higher than average. You will thus have more lucky numbers to explore!

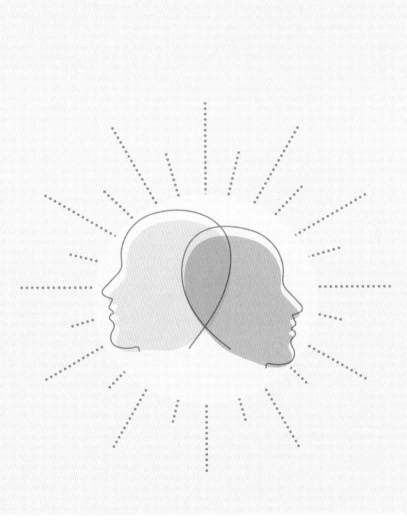

TRANSFORM YOUR WEAKNESSES INTO STRENGTHS

Use intuitive numerology and personality symbolism as self-development tools. To bask in the energy of your main personality type (and the lucky numbers associated to it), I invite you to read about it first. Then, in order to holistically balance your mind, read about the other personality types, one by one.

PLANNER

Your goal is to accept criticism

Here are my three solutions to help you better accept criticism:

- Be aware of the identity of the person giving you criticism. Others are but a mirror of ourselves, or at least a part of it. So, it is good to remember that criticism can reflect the image and energy of the person expressing it. Sometimes you are just a role in the story of the person criticizing you. Don't take anything personally.

- Analyze what is upsetting you internally. Do you find this criticism false, unfair, uncalled for? Does it echo your fears or beliefs?

- Look on the bright side, for not all criticism is bad. Some things can reveal themselves to be very positive, for they will push you to evolve by developing new skills.

SOCIABLE

Your goal is to accept solitude

- It's not always easy to accept solitude. And yet, no one but you can live your life for you. From the moment you are born until the moment you die, you are alone. So why not become your own friend instead of your enemy?

- Whether this moment of solitude is wanted or not, use it to get to know yourself better and understand what simply makes you happy. Happiness can be shared profusely, but it shouldn't be dependent on something external (a person, situation, or special place). Your environment and your entourage should only amplify your joy, not be the source of it. Dive in the depth of yourself and draw on your own inner resources to enjoy this tête-à-tête with yourself.

THINKER

Your goal is to let go

To let go and softly calm your thoughts, I invite you to comfortably sit down and close your eyes. Imagine that you are safely floating in a hot-air balloon. Little by little, it is rising in the sky. Look in the distance and focus on the horizon. The more you rise away from the ground, the lighter you will feel. Practice this short exercise whenever your thoughts get ahead of yourself like a hamster in its wheel. You may then let go more easily of your negative thoughts and burdening emotions.

LEADER

Your goal is active listening

Active listening is a great communication tool. It allows you to unlock conflictual relationships or to help with painful events. Active listening is based on comprehension, rephrasing and verification (or validation). That is why I like to call it the CRV technique.

- C is for comprehension. To help you better understand your interlocutor, it is essential to use open questioning. Open questions start with why, how, when, and which, and they cannot be replied to with yes or no. They open the door to sharing and dialogue.

- R is for rephrasing. Based on the answers you were given, I advise you to rephrase the words you heard in order to support the emotions they expressed. Observe how your interlocutor reacts. If they do not agree with what you said, go deeper with an open question.

- V is for verification or validation. Tutors and teachers know this last point very well, for it is essential for learning. It validates the good understanding and appropriation of the message. This verification (or validation) is essential before you can try to find solutions for your interlocutor.

Of course, this technique works only if your interlocutor is willing to answer you. If they are not, express your opinions by talking only about you and your feelings. The word you can be antagonizing. For instance, instead of saying "You drive me crazy when you do this," it is better to say "I feel X way when you do Y thing." No one can contradict your feelings if you express them with honesty and sincerity.

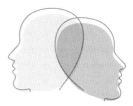

THE SYMBOLISM OF MIRROR HOURS

✧

In this part, I will reveal my nonexhaustive and symbolic interpretations of mirror hours. These can be very subjective. Just like with master number symbolism (p. 113), they resonate within me and echo with many of the people who consulted me. But if you don't agree with them, don't worry! It's absolutely inconsequential since—remember—intuitive numerology pushes us to discover and understand things in an unusual way. It can be unsettling if you are not used to it. So take all the time you need.

WHAT ARE MIRROR HOURS?

Have you ever stumbled across the terms mirror hours, twin hours, or double hours? Do you know what they really are? Many situations can apply to this phenomenon. For instance, someone asks you the time, you check your watch, a nearby clock catches your eye, or you find yourself in a place with the time on display. Then, you see "by chance" a double number! For example, 06:06, 10:10, and 21:21 (6:06 a.m., 10:10 a.m., and 9:09 p.m., respectively). Note that numerology uses the 24-hour clock, including zeroes before single-digit hours.

Many hypotheses have been said to explain this phenomenon, most of them connected to our subconscious. Time was divided by humans. Then, it corresponds to a subjective notion that doesn't mean anything after the transition. You may have been scarred and/or traumatized by an event at a very specific time, and you are reminded of this event regularly through your subconscious.

When some people see a mirror hour, they usually think that:

- Their guardian angel or a benevolent being of light is communicating with them.

- A person (deceased or not) is thinking about them.

- It is the answer to a question they had.

- It reflects their thoughts or state (physical, emotional, or relational) at the time.

- It will be lucky, and they immediately make a wish.

LISTEN TO YOURSELF!

When practicing intuitive numerology, trust your intuition. If my explanations don't "speak" to you and you don't feel anything while reading them, it probably means that this symbolism doesn't vibrate with your energy. You'll one day find other methods and techniques that will naturally resonate with you.

24 HOURS OF MIRROR HOURS

(MIDNIGHT)
THE TIME TO CHOOSE

Keywords: sacrifice, absence, waiting, silence, mental preparation, going backward, excess of control, forgetting oneself, spiritual awakening, and stopping.

My advice: Remember to think about yourself before focusing on others to offer them your help.

DOUBLE HOURS AND ENERGY 1:01, 1:11, and 11:11 strongly resonate with your energy and particularly with your vitality levels. If you come across these times while thinking (if you're not moving or have a poor health), leave the fertile soil of your mind and act.

(1:01 A.M.)
THE TIME TO REFLECT

Keywords: solitude, isolation, introspection, turning toward oneself, beginning, productive brainstorming, inspiration, ideas, and thinking about important plans.

My advice: Stay open-minded in order to take initiatives wisely.

(2:02 A.M.)
THE TIME FOR DUALITY

Keywords: inner struggle, antagonism, complementarity, seemingly impossible situation, important choice, and beneficial action.

My advice: Be attentive and show discernment.

03:03
(3:03 A.M.)
THE TIME TO COMMUNICATE

Keywords: thought, willpower, sharing, creativity, abundant ideas, expression, and active listening.
My advice: In order to not attract jealousy, be discreet about your projects, dreams and goals.

05:05
(5:05 A.M.)
THE TIME TO CREATE

Keywords: life, co-creation of your life, transmission, activity, vitality, great energy reserve, and natural ability to heal through magnetism (applying your hands).
My advice: Keep your feet firmly planted on the floor, and avoid being hyperactive.

04:04
(4:04 A.M.)
THE TIME FOR THE NATURAL LAW

Keywords: natural cycles, government, power, shape, strength, earth, personal qualities and assets, important spiritual improvement, and letting go.
My advice: Watch out for a particular situation, person, or event.

06:06
(6:06 A.M.)
THE TIME FOR WISDOM

Keywords: harmony, intuition, loyalty, choice, ability to learn quickly, and beneficial spiritual evolution.
My advice: Be at peace with yourself and let go of all the troubling things that drag you down.

THE POWER OF 11

The mirror hour 11:11 (11:11 a.m.) has inspired many artists, like the director of *Saw*, Darren Lynn Bousman. His movie *11-11-11* came out on November 11, 2011. This date wasn't picked at random, since his movie is about 11:11, gathering people fascinated by this mirror hour. Fascinated by the master number 11, I learned while doing some research that this director was born on January 11! There's really no such thing as a coincidence!

(7:07 A.M.)
THE TIME FOR REALIZATION

Keywords: gratification, encouragement, ancestral knowledge, confirmation of inspiring ideas, spirituality, association, and constant but gradual evolution.
My advice: Confidently and serenely keep going.

DOUBLE HOURS AND FAMILY 08:08, 08:18, and 18:18 (8:08 a.m., 8:18 a.m., and 6:18 p.m.) invite you to analyze the current relationships in your family. When you stumble upon these mirror hours, it means you are on the path to healing through separation, especially with these people.

(8:08 A.M.)

The time for freedom
Keywords: great life chance, ethics, law, discipline, consciousness, and spiritual power.
My advice: Get closer to the people who trust you. They will be of great help.

(9:09 A.M.)

The time for doubt
Keywords: complexity, uncertainty, indecisiveness, doubt, fear of being wrong, inner life, humanitarianism, and new friendship.
My advice: If you don't know where you stand, be careful and recover your inner balance.

(10:10 A.M.)

The time for realization

Keywords: self-confidence, luck, work, elevation, intuition, happy and fulfilled life, accomplishments, abundance, and greed.

My advice: Be aware of your free will and your ability to co-create. You have everything you need to succeed.

> **DID YOU KNOW?** 11:11 and 22:22 (11:11 a.m. and 10:22 p.m.) are the mirror hours people see the most.

(11:11 A.M.)

The time to be inspired

Keywords: charisma, appealing (physically and intellectually), seduction, great novel ideas, visionary, thirst for power, nervousness, self-sacrifice, and rebellion.

My advice: Keep a cool head even if your sudden glory is exhilarating!

(12:12 P.M.)

The time for a formative challenge

Keywords: clairvoyance, karma, lucky charm, spirituality, discernment, intuition, willful renunciation, and enlightened decision-making.

My advice: Develop your medium abilities at your rhythm.

13:13
(1:13 P.M.)

The time for cyclical mutation
Keywords: taste for chance, renewal, death, grief, rebirth, inner strength, changing your daily life, beneficial evolution, and novelty.

My advice: Listen to your inner voice, for it is giving you precious advice.

15:15
(3:15 P.M.)

The time for passion
Keywords: emotion, richness of heart, infatuation, sensibility, sexuality, magnetic power, energy, willpower, and regression.

My advice: Deal with your libido and infatuation in a healthy way.

14:14
(2:14 P.M.)

The time for instability
Keywords: intensity, progress, motion, involution, self-doubt and doubting others, renunciation, and loss of confidence after a failure.

My advice: Be careful not to scatter yourself, and refocus your energy in order to serenely find your balance again.

16:16
(4:16 P.M.)

The time for purification
Keywords: pride, arrogance, isolation, deep introspection, letting go, solitude, clearing your mind, letting go of materialistic worries, and reconnecting with nature.

My advice: Do a big clean up, internal and external.

17:17
(5:17 P.M.)

The time for purification
Keywords: creative force, will to surpass oneself, intense energy, inner strength, creativity, intense emotions, passionate feelings, and gratitude.
My advice: Remember to focus on the goals you set for yourself. You're on the right path to accomplish them.

> **DOUBLE HOURS AND PAST LIVES** 17:17 and 07:17 (5:17 p.m. and 7:17 a.m.) strongly resonate with your past lives. Whether it is a present action relying on a knowledge or experience you had in your past life, or a pathway opening to another dimension.

18:18
(6:18 P.M.)

The time for magic
Keywords: the realization of your wishes, the power of synchronicity, love, receptiveness, letting go of the things that don't work anymore, illusions, and pretentiousness.
My advice: Keep believing in yourself and your heart's desires.

19:19
(7:19 P.M.)

The time for purification
Keywords: fertile energy, universal light, renewal, release, life-saving transformation, need for metamorphosis, and positive visualization.
My advice: Be patient and determined. Pay attention to your dreams.

20:20
(8:20 P.M.)

The time for a roller coaster
Keywords: rapidity, intensity, ups and downs, the need to understand things, the need for discernment, open-mindedness, and favoring outside advice.

My advice: If you aren't fully happy with your life, change the way you think and adapt your attitude and how you behave.

22:22
(10:22 P.M.)

The time for promises
Keywords: intense preparation for prestige, fame and visibility, transforming your gifts into skills, beneficial waiting, shared love, and upcoming "miracle."

My advice: Be aware of the universe's plans. Some things need to be arranged before you can reach your goals.

21:21
(9:21 P.M.)

The time for success
Keywords: coronation, congratulations, good news, synthesis, divine wisdom, and beginning of a great personal accomplishment.

My advice: Take the first step and go for it. You won't regret it.

23:23
(11:23 P.M.)

The time for bravery
Keywords: dexterity, perseverance, determination, hard work, protection, communication, inheritance, and co-creation of a new project.

My advice: Work in joy today so your near future can be fulfilling.

RATIONAL NUMEROLOGY

INTUITIVE NUMEROLOGY

My active number: . . . . . .

My hereditary number: . . . .

My expression number: . . . . . .

My aspiration number: . . . . . .

My hidden self: . . . . . .

My spiritual initiation: . . . . . .

My force number: . . . . . .

My life path: . . . . . .

My personal year: . . . . . .

My current month: . . . . . .

My birth month: . . . . . .

My current day: . . . . . .

My birth day: . . . . . .

My favorite symbolism:

. . . .

My element is:

. . . .

My color is:

. . . .

My animal is:

. . . .

My personality is:

. . . .

CONCLUSION

"Words are the mysterious bystanders of the soul."
—Victor Hugo

This book about rational and intuitive numerology is my eighth solo book. This is no coincidence! The number 8 is a materialistic, ambitious, and combative builder, and it does not do things halfway, for its commitment value is particularly strong. Construction being at the core of its deep aspirations, the number 8 likes to create things that last in time. I thus sincerely hope that you enjoyed reading this book as much as I enjoyed writing it.

I don't believe that there is only one method to totally accept and follow blindly. That is why the goal of this book is first and foremost to invite you to explore the different numerology methods, but also to understand your brain's hemispheres in order to go into rational and intuitive numerology in depth.

We are all unique and different. Throughout our life, we evolve, we enrich and transform ourselves. Our truth today could be drastically different tomorrow, or it could stay the same. There are no mistakes, no failures, simply life experiences.

By reading this book, know that you have only walked a small fraction of the beautiful path of numerology. From now on, it's up to you to walk further. It's up to you to practice, to try all these different methods. My only advice is to always surpass the limits of your knowledge. Learning is constantly understanding and questioning ourselves in order expend out of our comfort zone.

I wish you a practice filled with experiences and discoveries.
Never forget that you are the co-creator of your life. You control your
destiny . . . so, it's up to you!

ACKNOWLEDGMENTS

Many thanks to . . .

All the people who have helped in the making of this book, from both sides of the Atlantic, and especially to my editor, Vanessa, for her trust.

Anabelle, for her precious proofreading and her loyalty since day one.

Matthieu Fortin, my editor from Quebec, who has helped me write my first book on numerology.

My husband, my most loyal proofreader.

My guides of light.

All the honest, kind, and professional people I have met for the past ten years, in all the different self-development fields. But also to all the jealous, envious, and manipulative people who have crossed my path.

All the people who have helped this book, directly or indirectly. Like Aurélie, who introduced me to numerology during a dinner out of time, but also Bouchera, my dear friend and numerology colleague.

All the people who didn't believe in me in the past, today, or even tomorrow. Thank you to all the people who, on the contrary, trust me blindly.

And finally, a great *thank you* to someone you know well: you! Without readers, there's no writer!

ABOUT THE AUTHOR

Anne-Sophie Casper is a Reiki master, teacher, licensed massage therapist, certi-
fied coach, and energy specialist. She is the author of oracles as well as personal
growth and well-being books, and the host of conferences, training sessions, and a
radio column on self-development. A numerologist trained in several recognized
methods, she hosts courses and seminars for others who would like to learn.

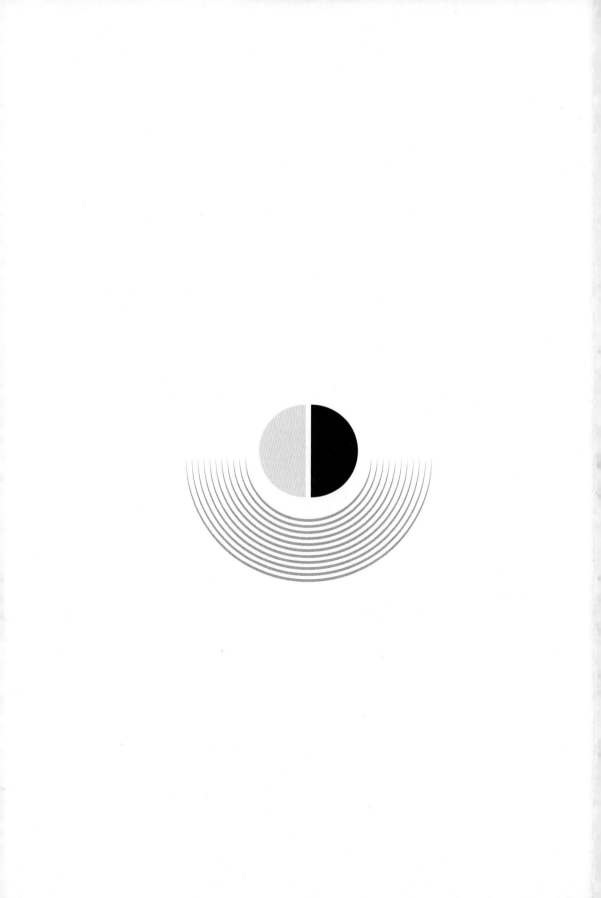